THE CENTERS OF CIVILIZATION SERIES

D0760340

# AIX-LA-CHAPELLE

## IN THE AGE OF CHARLEMAGNE

# aix-la-chapelle
## IN THE AGE OF CHARLEMAGNE

by *Richard E. Sullivan*

UNIVERSITY OF OKLAHOMA PRESS

*Norman*

Library of Congress Catalog Card Number: 63–18076

*Aix-la-Chapelle in the Age of Charlemagne* is Volume 10 in *The Centers of Civilization Series*.

*To Liz • Kate • and Mimi*
ALL OF WHOM MIGHT HAVE ENDEARED
THEMSELVES TO CHARLEMAGNE

# PREFACE

IN KEEPING WITH the rationale of the series of which it is a part, this book is intended as an interpretation rather than as a history of an era. It is based on the conviction that through an acquaintance with typical activities transpiring in the city of Aix-la-Chapelle during the age of Charlemagne, defined as the period from 790 to 840, a reader can gain insight into the fundamental nature of a crucial historical era. In order to highlight what seems vital to the age of Charlemagne, I have had to choose from the vast variety of details that constitute the totality of Carolingian history. My choices have constantly been guided by a desire to emphasize what men in the age of Charlemagne placed first in their lives, hoping that such a procedure would keep the reader as much as possible in direct contact with the temper and spirit of the era. Often this approach has led me to neglect what other specialists might consider essential to Carolingian history and what I myself would certainly include in a "history" of the age of Charlemagne.

I hope especially that my interpretation of the age of Charlemagne will provoke in my readers a deeper interest in a broad problem which is essential to a full comprehension of the history of Western European civilization. I find it difficult to dissociate the age of Charlemagne from the larger subject of the origin and initial configuration of the Western European tradition. Before beginning this book, a reader may find it profitable to consider what he himself recalls about the beginning and basic ingredients of the European cultural tradition. In the pages that follow he will be confronted with suggestions about this crucial issue. For it is my contention that the age of Charlemagne has a special place in the history of Europe that has not always been fully appreciated. Whatever the validity of my position, I hope that my suggestions relative to this vital historiographical question will stimulate new understanding in each reader and will aid in a substantial way in shaping his total historical perspective.

Throughout the book I have used the name "Aix-la-Chapelle" for Charlemagne's city. In no way is this decision intended as a slight to modern Aachen. Aix-la-Chapelle has simply seemed to be a better rendering of the Latin usage prevailing in Carolingian sources.

This book owes a great deal to a number of modern authorities on Carolingian history. The format of the series precludes giving recognition to each, but I trust that this general acknowledgment of my debt to them will convey some of my gratitude. I especially wish to thank Monsignor E. Stephany, *Domvikar* at Aachen, and Professor F. L. Ganshof of the University of Ghent for their helpful suggestions. To Professor J. F. A. Taylor of Michigan State University I am especially grateful for his intelligent reading of parts of the manuscript. To President Charles E. Odegaard of the University of Washington, who once talked of writing such a book before being called to other responsibilities, I owe more than can be adequately expressed here. During the preparation of this book I benefitted from the assistance of the staffs of the library of Michigan State University, of the library of the University of Louvain, and of the Bibliothèque Royale in Brussels. My work has profited immensely from an opportunity to see modern Aachen at first hand and to study many documents —especially art works—in their original form. As a Fulbright research scholar in Belgium in 1961–62 and as a John Simon Guggenheim fellow I was able to see and study the necessary documents. Finally, to my wife, Vivian Johnson Sullivan, I owe an immense debt of gratitude for more than can be listed here.

*Richard E. Sullivan*

EAST LANSING, MICHIGAN

# CONTENTS

xiii

# AIX-LA-CHAPELLE

## IN THE AGE OF CHARLEMAGNE

# PROLOGUE

𝔞 THIRTEENTH-CENTURY HYMN opened with these words: *"Sing, city of Aix, regal city,/ Chief seat of the kingdom,/ First court of kings . . . ."* An author proposing to present the city of Aix-la-Chapelle as a center of civilization would like to assume that these majestic words might kindle in his readers' minds a recollection of some past age of glory which would immediately explain why the book in hand was undertaken. If Rome, Athens, Constantinople, or Paris were substituted for Aix, there would be no doubt. In writing of Aix, one cannot expect such easy access to his readers' minds. He must enter a special plea justifying and explaining his effort.

We habitually tend to equate the greatness and significance of a city with the length of time that it enjoyed a leading role in history. In many instances this criterion has undoubted merit. Everyone can recall many cities whose central position in history is measured in terms of a millennium or more: Memphis, Thebes, Babylon, Knossus, Jerusalem, Athens, Rome, Paris, London, Constantinople, Baghdad, and Venice. Even the youthful cities of the world —New York, Moscow, Berlin, Tokyo, Washington, Buenos Aires, and New Delhi—have acquired a certain patina to hide their muscular challenge to the older centers of civilization. Barring some not impossible cataclysm, these teeming centers seem destined to serve for centuries as foci of creativity and to provide further proof that longevity is a mark of a city's greatness.

However, a reflective student of history will realize that the historical role of some cities cannot be assessed in years. Who would essay to recount the history of mankind without allotting a place of importance to Medina in the years between 622 and 630, Samarkand in the days of Tamerlane's glory, Bruges in the fourteenth century, Ravenna in the sixth century, Pella in the era of Philip of Macedon and Alexander the Great, Toulouse in the twelfth century, or Karakorum in the ominous years of Ghengis Khan? Yet time in centuries offers no clue to the place of these cities in history.

If longevity fails to provide an explanation of the importance of a certain category of city in history, perhaps the solution lies in some kind of relationship between the city and the historical setting. A little reflection on the place of the cities just listed in the grand sweep of history will suggest that each stood temporally and spatially at a crucial juncture when radical changes occurred affecting the historical scene for centuries. Each played a brief but highly significant role as a center from which issued the basic impulses at once causing and heralding a radical deviation in the trajectory of historical events.

This cursory speculation on the essential characteristics of cities which have been crucial in history suggests a dual classification. Into one group falls those cities which are products of the complex energies and achievements of a civilization that has reached a mature stage. The pattern of life that unfolds in such cities embraces the successful

4

answers that a creative society has found to the whole range of problems confronting men as social creatures. Because they are products of the ultimate achievements of the society which builds them, these cities enjoy a stable career that extends over generations and even centuries. A second group consists of cities which serve momentarily as receptacles for men and ideas engaged in the act of changing the course of human affairs. By the very nature of things these cities are destined to enjoy fame briefly; the revolutionary forces initiated within their confines soon sweep them into oblivion and distribute the laurels among other cities that flourish by exploiting the changed situation.

Aix-la-Chapelle belongs to the second category. For only a short period during the half-century from 790 to 840 was its role of fundamental importance. Yet during these years —the age of Charlemagne—it was the center of a series of actions which caused a basic shift in the course of human affairs. This moment was long enough to leave a permanent impression on Western European civilization, a mark not too well appreciated or understood by those schooled to seek the origins of Western European civilization in classical antiquity or in the Renaissance and Reformation.

The most revealing clue to Aix's precise role as the scene of a fundamental change in the course of history is supplied by the ambivalence that still surrounds its name. On today's maps it is designated by the unmistakably Germanic name, Aachen; however, not very long ago it was known by an obviously French name, Aix-la-Chapelle. This duality points to the fact that Aachen or Aix-la-Chapelle lies along a frontier between two segments of European society whose encounters have been decisive in Western European history—between the Germanic and the Gallic, the Teutonic and the Latin worlds.

To raise the specter of the meeting of the Germanic and the Latin worlds may serve to unsettle rather than to illuminate the reader's mind. For who can contemplate that encounter without a myriad of impressions, most of them overlaid with strong emotional tones? One's mind races across a multitude of unpleasant events ranging from the hate-filled, murderous, city-leveling wars of the last hundred years to the arrogant triumphal marches of Roman military giants who two thousand years ago returned to the proud city on the Tiber displaying their cowering barbarian captives seized along the northern fringes of the civilized world. These recollections, smelling of gore and destruction, almost convince one that one of history's prime tragedies has been the meeting of Teutons and Latins.

Yet the encounter of the Germanic and Latin worlds had a positive, constructive side that produced creative, civilizing consequences immensely more significant than the violent clashes that have made such an impression on most of us. It was Aix-la-Chapelle's role to serve during a brief half-century as a center where men consciously sought to combine Germanic and Latin elements to form a new society and where they garnered the first fruits of that synthesis. During the reigns of the renowned Charlemagne (768–814) and his son Louis the Pious (814–840), Aix became a focal point for an effort by a remarkable circle of men inspired with a powerful urge to roll back the barbarism that had settled over Europe during the era following the collapse of Roman civilization and the migrations of the barbaric Germans. Their assault on barbarism

6

hardly resolved all the ills of the age, but their methods, ideas, and successes went far to re-establish the foundations of orderly, purposeful, and civilized life. On the foundations which they constructed Western European civilization developed—rapidly, when one views the totality of human history—to a position of supremacy in the world scene.

In the pages that follow the chief aim, then, is to employ the events that occurred in Aix in the age of Charlemagne as a mirror reflecting the drama of the creative meeting of the Germanic and the Latin worlds in a chaotic setting. Whenever possible we shall permit contemporaries to tell what was happening, why they thought it was happening, and what they hoped would result. We trust that a verbal reconstruction of life in a single city which served as a foyer of a nascent society will open new vistas to those who experience excitement in comprehending those vital pulsations which indicate radical changes in the historical process. And we think that if our effort reveals that Aix-la-Chapelle was the scene of a fundamental shift in the course of history, we are more than justified in calling it a center of civilization.

# one

## THE LARGER SCENE

THE SUGGESTION that Aix-la-Chapelle's role as a center of civilization depended on its relationship to a particularly pregnant historical moment assumes meaning only in terms of the profound changes which characterized the eighth century. The effort to understand these developments plunges us into a tangled set of relationships affecting the entire Mediterranean basin.

As the eighth century opened, three extensive cultural areas confronted each other around the Mediterranean: the Byzantine Empire, the Moslem Empire, and the Germanic Western European world. All three had emerged as by-products of the complex process marking the collapse of the Roman Empire and the end of the unity that the Romans had imposed on the diverse population living around the Mediterranean. There is not space here to recount the long chain of events which between 400 and 700 led from Roman unity to the tripartition of the Mediterranean basin. What is important is that by 700 differences between the Byzantine, Moslem, and Germanic worlds, coupled with unique forces operating within each, created a situation which generated rapid and revolutionary changes during the eighth century.

Two decisive military engagements signaled the first profound change of the eighth century. During the winter of

717–18 the Byzantine Empire repulsed a furious land and sea assault on Constantinople conducted by Moslem forces. Fourteen years later, in 732, a Frankish force led by Charles Martel successfully blocked a Moslem bid for mastery of Gaul by crushing a Moslem army in a battle fought near Poitiers (often mistakenly called the "Battle of Tours").

These two engagements marked a turning point in Moslem history. For a century before 732, Moslem expansionism had provided the chief dynamic element in the Mediterranean area. The emergence of Moslem power in the world scene represented an incredible chapter in history. The ancestors of the Moslem soldiers engaged at Constantinople and Poitiers had only a century earlier been nomadic tribesmen living a poverty-stricken, semibarbarian life in the Arabian desert and exercising virtually no influence on the larger world. Out of this environment emerged a remarkable man, Mohammed (c.570–632), a prophet who bequeathed his fellow Arabs a new religion, called Islam. Islam served as a chrysalis which transmuted the disorganized Arab tribesmen into empire builders and creators of a new civilization. United as soldiers of Allah, the Arabs boiled out of their restrictive desert environment to lay hands on the lands and riches, techniques and ideas of surrounding civilizations. Quickly they fashioned a vast empire stretching eastward to India and Turkestan and westward across North Africa into Spain. The Mediterranean sea became a Moslem sea. The Persian Empire succumbed completely before this onslaught, the Byzantine Empire lost its richest possessions—Syria, Palestine, Egypt, and North Africa—and numerous less prominent nations passed under the Arab yoke. The Moslem push across Asia

9

Minor to the walls of Constantinople and the thrust into Gaul early in the eighth century appeared to presage new and even more spectacular successes.

At Constantinople and Poitiers the Moslems were defeated—a rare occurrence in previous Moslem history. These setbacks were harbingers of the end of Arab expansion and of the shifting of Moslem society towards new pursuits destined to relieve the non-Moslem world of the danger of conquest and to transform the inner structure of Moslem society. Internal political trouble, caused by overextension of the empire and by discontent with the privileges enjoyed by the dominant Arab minority over their non-Arab subjects, led to a crisis in 750. The Umayyad dynasty, which had ruled since 661 and which had fostered aggressive militarism and Arab domination, was replaced by a new dynasty, the Abbasids. The new rulers pursued a policy which reduced Arab influence and which made religion rather than ethnic origin the key to full membership in Moslem society. The loosening of the iron rule of the militant Arabs bred political separatism and heralded the disintegration of the unified caliphate into competing Moslem states. These internal disturbances blunted Moslem expansionism, ending at long last the Moslem menace to other peoples.

Abbasid rule brought a new kind of power and splendor to the Moslem world. After 750 the dynamism of Moslem society was directed toward the refinement and enrichment of the vast empire internally. The new orientation manifested itself in resplendent cities, flourishing trade, world-renowned skills in handicrafts, magnificent mosques, and impressive achievements in philosophy, science, theology, and literature. The maturation of Moslem civilization after 750 provided the entire world with a new standard of material and cultural excellence; the debt of neighboring societies was immense. In 750, however, the changing face of Islam had a more immediate and direct import; it removed the incessant threat of conquest offered by the more militant soldiers of Allah who had directed Moslem destiny before that time.

No less significant than the end of Moslem expansionism in the total configuration of the eighth century were changes in the orientation of the Byzantine world. The Byzantine Empire had originated as the direct successor of the universal Roman Empire; its beginnings might be placed in 330, when Emperor Constantine shifted the capital of the empire to Constantinople. But in making this change, Constantine in no sense abandoned any of the authority claimed by his predecessors. He and his successors claimed universal dominion over the Mediterranean world; theirs was the duty of sustaining the Pax Romana in its political, economic, cultural, and spiritual aspects. Men were convinced in the fourth century that Rome was eternal, and so they remained in Constantinople for many centuries.

In actuality, the rulers of Constantinople retained their universal power in the Mediterranean world only briefly. The Germanic invasions of the fifth century reduced the "universal" Roman Empire to an "eastern" Roman Empire; after the Germanic migrations had ceased, the lords of Constantinople retained only part of Italy and North Africa in the West. Throughout the sixth and seventh centuries the eastern remnant of old Rome was subjected to new assaults, chiefly from the east and north. These attacks inexorably pared away vital territories previously claimed by Constantinople. Extensive areas of the Balkans south of the Danube were occupied by Slavs, who usually moved into Roman territory after the authority of the emperor had already been undermined by the victorious forays of Asiatic nomads, such as the Avars and the Bulgars. The emperors successfully stood off Persian assaults in Syria and Palestine in the sixth century only to see this vital area, along with Egypt and North Africa, fall to the Arabs in the seventh century. By the opening of the eighth century it was no longer realistic to call the surviving remnant of the old Roman Empire an "eastern Roman Empire." It had been reduced to a rather modest state comprising the southern Balkan peninsula and Asia Minor with a tenuous outpost in Italy. Even what remained under Constantinople's sway was precariously held, as the already noted Arab offensive in the early eighth century indicated.

The incessant pressure on the frontiers of the Roman Empire from the fifth to the eighth century had not only reduced its size but also slowly transformed its inner structure. Historians seek to capture the essence of this change in a succinct fashion by saying that the old "Roman" Empire became a "Byzantine" Empire. By using this terminology, they mean many things. Ethnically the empire lost its cosmopolitan character and became predominantly Greek. Political and social institutions were altered in response to military pressures until they took a form distinct from their Roman archetypes. Culturally, the new society shed its Latin aspects and found its basis in the cultural heritage of ancient Greece and the Hellenistic world. Even the Christian religion of the emergent Byzantine world assumed institutional, theological, moral, and spiritual patterns that were unique. Although the connections reaching back to old Rome were never abruptly or consciously severed, the pressures of time and circumstance had by 700 left little in Constantinople or the territory under its sway that was, properly speaking, Roman.

The great crisis of 717–18 resulted in a further transformation of Byzantine society so serious in its total import that reverberations were felt far beyond Byzantine boundaries. The Arab siege of Constantinople brought to the imperial throne an Armenian general named Leo III. After establishing himself as a savior of Byzantium through his leadership in relieving the siege of Constantinople and still not aware that the Moslem thrust had spent itself, Leo III instituted a series of reforms aimed at providing new military resources to insure Byzantium's future safety and to liberate Asia Minor. His solution was to entrust the military burden to the peasants of Asia Minor, who were rewarded with modest farms safeguarded from the depredations of great landowners by the authority of the emperor. This step made Asia Minor the hub of the empire and marked a serious compromise with imperial claims of universality.

The implementation of the new military policy necessitated administrative changes designed to strengthen the power of military commanders at the expense of civilian bureaucrats and to exalt still further the power of the emperor to the disadvantage of the factious but cosmopolitan aristocracy clustered around the imperial court. The ascendancy of the military-peasant element brought a subtle change to the mentality guiding Byzantine society. Nowhere was this new spirit more evident than in Leo's religious reforms. Acting partly from a strongly puritanical personal inclination and partly from a desire to curb the growing power of certain segments of the ecclesiastical world—especially the monks—Leo issued an edict in 726 prohibiting the employment of statues (icons) in religious services and in church decoration. When his order was resisted, he countered with stringent measures aimed at purging the church of the "image worshipers." The consequence was a struggle which became the predominant issue of eighth-century Byzantine history. The bitter quarrel between the iconoclasts and the iconodules, to which many other issues became attached, undermined the effectiveness of the government and sapped the authority of the emperors. The iconoclastic position brought charges of heresy from Christians outside the empire, especially in Western Europe, and thus acerbated the religious differences which had already begun to divide Eastern and Western Christians. Embroiled in these internal problems and oriented irrevocably toward a military-political regime based on Asia Minor and the East, Byzantium increasingly withdrew from the world scene as the eighth century progressed. Consequently the empire lost stature as Rome's direct and universal successor, a development which encouraged others to challenge Byzantine claims to that role and to assume it themselves.

No doubt the transformations affecting the Moslem and Byzantine worlds were connected with the third and most impressive change characterizing the eighth century— the resurgence of the Germanic West. The revival of the West came somewhat as a surprise, for prior to 700 the Western world had experienced a troubled era that historians justly term the "dark age." The Germanic invaders who partitioned the Roman West in the fifth century hardly distinguished themselves as upholders of civilized life. Political disorder prevailed everywhere, nourished by the division of the West among several ruthlessly aggressive Germanic kingdoms and by the inability of the Germanic monarchs to sustain orderly governmental processes within their "states." In spite of their initial efforts to imitate Roman political institutions, the Germanic kings could not divest themselves of barbarian concepts of government which emphasized rule by force. Slowly the idea of the state as an agency responsible for public welfare and for service to its citizens was eroded by kings and their warrior companions who approached political life from a private or dynastic point of view. Economic life retrogressed as a result of political disorder and a decline of trade and technical skills. City life deteriorated as society shifted toward agricultural pursuits. Moral, spiritual, intellectual, and artistic life suffered gradual barbarization, leaving the West inferior to the more robust, sophisticated societies of the Byzantine and Moslem empires. Here and there in the West there were developments which indicated that conditions were not completely hopeless. But these tentative, experimental moves toward a new order did not offset the prevailing climate of disorder, decay, barbarization, and chaos. Caught up in its "dark age," the West seemed hardly worthy of being ranked with Byzantium and the Moslems as a partner among civilized societies.

Yet this over-all complexion of Western society was misleading, for constructive forces existed amidst the general chaos. One such force showed forth at the Battle of Poitiers in the person of Charles Martel, who represented the emergence of an energetic dynasty capable of providing decisive leadership over the most potent political entity in the West, the Frankish kingdom, and of releasing the potential of the most creative institution in the West, the Church.

The Franks had emerged as a leading force in the West during the period of the Germanic invasions. Under their first great king, Clovis (486–511), and his immediate successors, they had through conquest erected a formidable kingdom embracing Gaul and a belt of Germanic territory east of the Rhine not previously part of the Roman Empire. This kingdom was unique among the other Germanic kingdoms formed in the era of the invasions because of the unusually large number of Germanic peoples joined with the conquered Gallo-Roman population under a single ruler. The Franks further enhanced their position during Clovis' reign by embracing the orthodox Christianity of the Roman population in the West at a time when most other Germanic dynasties militantly adhered to Arianism. The dynasty of Clovis, the Merovingians, seemed to offer hope that the transition from Roman to Germanic overlordship would be relatively painless in a large sector of the West. That the Franks instinctively sensed the central role thrust on them by the extent and location of their conquests is reflected in the prologue to one of their ancient law codes, which speaks of "the illustrious nation of the Franks, created by God, courageous in war, faithful to their promises in times of peace, wise in their decisions, noble in body, healthy, fair of skin, distinguished in appearance, bold, prompt, tenacious, converted to the catholic faith, free from all heresy . . . , the powerful nation which shook off the heavy yoke of the Romans with the aid of its courage and its tenacity."

Yet the Merovingians failed to sustain their early promise. By the end of the seventh century a desperate crisis embraced the Frankish kingdom and threatened its very existence. Royal authority had declined to a point where the kings were contemptuously called "do-nothing" kings. The once-unified kingdom had broken into four sub-kingdoms ruled over by various members of the Merovingian family. These petty kings and their entourages engaged in unending and murderous civil wars which engendered violence, injustice, and neglect of public responsibilities. The impotence of the kings encouraged separatism among non-Frankish groups which had earlier been incorporated in the Frankish kingdom by conquest. Everywhere public functions were usurped by great landowners, whose increasing power and independence represented a leading feature of the dark age in the West. By virtue of their control of large blocs of land the great proprietors gained a virtual monopoly over wealth in an age of vanishing trade and city life. They increasingly forced the peasantry into a position of hereditary dependency which obligated them to till the noble's land, a status not entirely unwelcome to the weak amidst the insecurity of the era. The lords assumed the rights and privileges of government over their estates and their dependents. The weak, embattled kings were increasingly forced to call on the nobles to perform public functions at private expense and rewarded them with grants of land and control over public offices. The mounting ambitions of the nobles had by the end of the seventh century reached the point where they were posed for a final assault on the remnants of royal power and wealth. Nothing seemed capable of saving the Frankish kingdom.

Out of this crisis emerged a Frankish aristocratic family, the Carolingians, capable of rehabilitating Frankish monarchy. The Carolingians originated in the area between the Meuse and the Rhine rivers in the sub-kingdom known as Austrasia. During the seventh century the family, already in possession of extensive landholdings, became mayors of the palace for the Merovingian kings of Austrasia, exploiting that office to enrich themselves and to build a loyal following among other aristocratic families in the area. After 650 the Carolingians enlarged their ambitions by seeking to gain control over the office of mayor of the palace in two other sub-kingdoms, Neustria and Burgundy, an ambition that engaged them in deadly rivalry with other aristocrats in quest of the same end. The real issue of this struggle was control over the resources of the crown, still claimed in theory by the "do-nothing" Merovingians. It was decided on the field of battle in 687 when the Carolingian mayor of the palace, Pepin of Heristal, smashed his chief rival, the mayor of the palace of Neustria. Pepin's victory placed the Carolingians in a position to claim authority over the whole kingdom and provided the point of departure for the reintegration of the Frankish state under a single authority.

The first two Carolingian mayors of the palace after 687, Pepin of Heristal (687–714) and Charles Martel (714–41), exploited the victory of 687 skillfully to build sturdy foundations for their successors. They devoted themselves dog-

gedly to an assault on three problems largely responsible
for the political chaos of previous generations: the lawless
independence of the landed aristocracy, the separatist ten-
dencies of certain sectors of the Frankish state, and dangerous ingressions into the Frankish state by foreigners.
Although their methods were often ruthless and heavy-
handed, their persistent efforts ultimately brought increasing order to society and a new respect for the authority of
the central government. In spite of their success, neither
Pepin nor Charles Martel bore any more exalted title than
mayor of the palace, theoretically serving the Merovingian
king. But mayors of the palace were kings in all but name.

The next mayor of the palace was emboldened by the
successes of his predecessors to take a major step in favor
of his dynasty—the transfer of the crown from the Merovingians to the Carolingians. Pepin the Short (741–68), the
son of Charles Martel, had the brute strength to achieve
this end, but was sagacious enough to realize that so drastic
a break with tradition needed legitimization. To sanction
his usurpation, Pepin resorted to a solution which had
monumental consequences for Western European society.
In 749 he sent two emissaries to Pope Zacharius asking
whether or not it was good to have kings with no power.
"The Pope answered Pepin that it was better that he be
called king who had power than he who reigned without
royal power; so that order should not be disturbed, he ordered through apostolic authority that Pepin be made
king." Thus justified, Pepin deposed the last Merovingian
in 751 and was himself elected king "according to the custom of the Franks." At his coronation a papal legate bestowed on him a special consecration.

The events surrounding the dynastic change in 751 represented a crucial step in the developing union between the Carolingians and the most dynamic elements of the Church, a coalition that provided much of the inspiration and energy for the revival of the West. For at the moment when Pepin decided to change dynasties, the Church was making notable progress in repairing some of the scars left on the spiritual countenance of Europe during the "dark age." The fifth, sixth, and seventh centuries were years marked by both success and difficulty for the Church. On the balance, one would probably have to decide that religious life suffered a general decline between 400 and 700, especially if one uses as a standard the religious aspirations and practices reflected by the great Latin fathers—Augustine, Jerome, Ambrose—or by the famous pastors—John Cassian, Caesarius of Arles, Martin of Tours—of the late Roman period. The decay of religious life in the "dark age" was especially marked in certain areas: the secularization of the clergy, the paganization of doctrine and liturgy, the decline of the intellectual level of the clergy, the neglect of pastoral duties, and the dislocation of the ecclesiastical organization. All through the "dark age" elements within the clergy and outside it combated these evils. Especially persistent in the struggle to sustain spiritual life against the relentless tide of barbarism were the papacy and the Benedictine monks, and it was they who buttressed the rising Carolingians so effectively in the eighth century.

The position of the papacy at the beginning of the eighth century was the result of an extremely complex chain of events reaching back almost to the origins of Christianity. At the risk of oversimplification, it might be said that prior

to the end of the fifth century the bishops of Rome had
formulated an ideology of their universal authority over
the Christian community in the form of the Petrine theory
and had enjoyed considerable success in exercising that
authority by virtue of their action in defense of orthodoxy
during the era of the great dogmatic disputes between 300
and 500. These initial successes were, however, seriously
compromised by the unheavals accompanying the fall of
Rome which operated to isolate the popes and to impede
the exercise of their universal authority. The intrusion of
Germanic invaders into Italy in the fifth and sixth centuries
threatened to impose barbarian domination on the popes.
When the imperial government in Constantinople finally
re-established imperial control over Rome during the reign
of Justinian (527–65), the bishops of Rome found themselves at the mercy of a "protector" who expected them
to act as simple territorial bishops responsible to the central
authority in the "second Rome." More influential in religious affairs of the Byzantine Empire was the patriarch of
Constantinople, who emerged as a serious challenger to
the universal authority claimed by the bishops of Rome.
In the Germanic West the Church tended to break into
"national" units gravitating around the Germanic monarchs. Finally, the Moslem conquests severed communications between Rome and the Christians of the Near East
and North Africa. In the increasingly fragmented world
of the sixth and seventh centuries the bishop of Rome was
left with extensive claims but narrowly limited effective
power.

Without abandoning Rome's universal claims, the papacy adjusted to the new situation by orienting its policy

toward the Western European scene. The architect of this new orientation was Pope Gregory I, the Great (590–604). Through careful exploitation of papal lands in Italy he attempted to create a material base for greater independence of action. In his extensive Latin writings Gregory restated many aspects of the Christian faith in a simplified form suitable to the mentality of the increasingly unsophisticated society of the West, earning for himself recognition as a new church father. Especially epoch-making was his decision to convert the pagan Anglo-Saxons of England under papal direction. To achieve this goal, he enlisted the services of Benedictine monks. This was a momentous choice, for the Benedictines represented a new regenerative force in the West. Their communal life was based on a rule drawn up by an Italian aristocrat, Benedict of Nursia (c.480–547), who withdrew from worldly affairs to follow the ascetic life. Not satisfied with the existing customs governing ascetic life, he wrote his own rule. It emphasized obedience, discipline, and ordered regularity to be achieved through prayer, study, and manual labor. Under this rule Benedict's monastery at Monte Cassino became a model religious community capable of self-support and internal stability. The rule was soon widely imitated in the West. As its use spread, there emerged a corps of elite "servants of Christ," whose discipline, learning, and piety exemplified a superior level of Christian excellence. This new ecclesiastical aristocracy, backed by the corporate wealth earned by its own labor and dedicated to service, was ideally suited for missionary work. The monks which Gregory sent to England not only routed paganism, but also obediently followed Rome's instructions in organizing

22

religious life and introducing Roman practices. Before the seventh century had progressed far, England had become an ecclesiastical province of Rome. This attachment represented a more intimate kind of relationship than the papacy had previously enjoyed with any Germanic people. The English missionary venture opened new prospects for the application of papal energies in a world scene that had been radically changed by the dissolution of Roman imperial unity.

The pioneering program charted by Gregory the Great bore fruit slowly in the chaotic seventh century. But early in the eighth century events unfolded rapidly to raise new problems for the papacy and to offer fresh opportunities for the expansion of papal authority in the West, that is, to pursue the broad lines of Gregory I's policy.

The most fundamental development occurred in the area of Byzantine-papal relationships. Finding it necessary to strain every resource in the defense of its eastern frontier against the Moslem threat, the Byzantine government relaxed its hold on Italy. This situation left the papacy increasingly without a reliable protector. At the same time Byzantium's chief rival in Italy, the Lombards, became more aggressive, threatening to engulf Rome and to submit the papacy to an even less desirable master. The strain caused by Byzantium's increasing unreliability as a protector was intensified by the iconoclastic quarrel. The papacy took the stand that Leo III's condemnation of the use of icons was heretical. The popes certainly could not trust their destiny to heretics—especially weak heretics. There was little choice for the popes except to seek a new champion; the only direction to turn was that toward which

Gregory had earlier oriented papal policy—toward the West and the Germans.

The pressures operating in papal-Byzantine relationships and in Italy to force the papacy to seek a new protector were complemented by the increasing prospects before the papacy for an extension of its authority in the Germanic world. This opportunity represented the fruit of Gregory's labor to convert England a century earlier. The Christian establishment had flourished so vigorously in England that by the beginning of the eighth century it was the most vital religious center in the West. One by-product of the intense spiritual activity there was the generation of a missionary urge, centering especially in the Benedictine monasteries. Missionary zeal found an outlet toward the Continent, where there were still many Germanic pagans. Led by men like Willibrord and Boniface, a considerable number of English monks moved into an area reaching from Frisia southward along the east bank of the Rhine to Bavaria to preach, baptize, found monasteries, and organize ecclesiastical life on a firm basis. Hardly had they arrived when they hastened to Rome to seek authorization and guidance for their work. During the first half of the eighth century their zeal and industry, fortified by papal support and advice, won many converts and established an episcopal structure carefully subjected to Rome. A competent, pious, dedicated clergy—most of them products of English monasteries or newly established Continental monasteries— assumed the direction of religious life and supplied a model of ecclesiastical excellence.

This new religious establishment on the Continent opened still another area for the application of the ideals of the papacy and the Benedictine monks. For the Anglo-Saxon missionaries had not only sought the blessing of the papacy but also had asked and received the support of the rapidly rising Carolingian dynasty. As the work of conversion, organization, and purification proceeded around the fringes of the Frankish kingdom, it became increasingly obvious that the Frankish church itself was badly in need of reform. Soon after Charles Martel's death a series of Frankish church councils were held to redress this situation. The leading spirit in this reform movement was the already mentioned Anglo-Saxon missionary, Boniface, by now bearing the title of papal legate. The decisions of these synods, stressing improvement of the clergy, the strengthening of church organization, and the purification of popular religious life, bore the strong mark of Roman inspiration. The bishop of Rome could well expect a growing respect for his authority in the Frankish kingdom in the future.

When Pepin's legates came to Rome in 749 with their request, many forces dictated that it was to the papal advantage to defer to the wishes of the rising dynasty in the north. The already-cited papal reply to Pepin marked the first in a series of events which established an intimate link between Rome and the Carolingians. In 754, Pope Stephen II journeyed to Gaul to redeem the obligation Pepin owed him. In a solemn ceremony he personally reconsecrated Pepin, and, according to one account, "He forbade anyone, under pain of interdict and excommunication, ever to dare choose a king of another line than that of these princes whom divine piety has deigned to exalt, and who, through the intercession of the holy apostles, had been confirmed and consecrated by the hand of the benevolent pontiff, their vicar." No other ruler in the West could claim so exalted a position. Stephen also bestowed on Pepin the title of "*patricius* of the Romans," which implied that the Frankish ruler had an obligation to protect the Pope and the city of Rome. Even more significantly, the meeting resulted in a promise of Pepin to intervene in Italy to safeguard territory claimed by the papacy against the depredations of the Lombards. Faithful to this promise, the Frankish king led armies into Italy in 754 and 756 and defeated the Lombards. These expeditions resulted in the famous Donation of Pepin, a document which turned over to the papacy certain specified territories in Italy. The document became the legal basis for a papal state safeguarded by Frankish might. The union between the Carolingians and the papacy was now solidly established. The rapidly rising Frankish family had won a crown sanctioned by the highest authority in the West; with the crown went a vast responsibility as "the strong right arm" of the Church. The popes had gained a powerful protector, a new stronghold in Italy from which to practice their spiritual overlordship, and acceptance by the most powerful segment of the Germanic world of the idea that Rome was the source of the faith.

When Pepin's reign ended in 768, the chief elements of strength and vitality in the West—the Carolingian dynasty, its aristocratic supporters, the papacy, the reformed episcopacy, and the Benedictine monks—had become intimately linked through mutual interest and common ideas. Could these forces acting in unison elevate Western Europe from its long sojourn in barbarism? At this critical moment a man of strength arrived on the scene to lead the forces of reconstruction forward. He was Charlemagne, whose reign constituted one of those dramatic moments when the historical continuum is bent into a new path.

This is not the place to review in detail his accomplishments, since his record will form the substance of the chapters that follow. It is necessary, however, to establish that his remarkable career bred mounting confidence in the West that a new day had dawned. His biographer, Einhard, provides a clue to his impact on the contemporary scene. "For this king," he wrote, "the wisest and most highminded of all those who in that age ruled over the nations of the world, never refused to undertake or carry through what needed to be done on account of the labor involved nor withdrew from such tasks through fear." It was his intense activity, his willingness "to undertake or carry through what needed to be done," which supplied the basis for his growing fame. That activity extended into every realm of life. Charlemagne proved spectacularly successful as a military commander; in the words of Einhard, he "so nobly expanded the kingdom of the Franks, which was already great and strong when he received it from his father Pepin, that it was almost doubled." The sword was not Charlemagne's only concern. As his wars progressed successfully, he pushed forward other projects which simultaneously strengthened his kingdom and enhanced his reputation. He mounted an assault on the political disorders within his realm, seeking to institute a regime of peace, order, and concord. He devoted special attention to the spiritual condition of his subjects, attempting to purify existing religious practices and deepen contemporary spirituality. He moved with decision to end the cultural decay

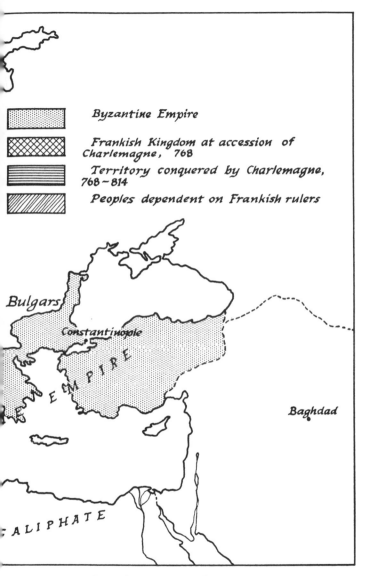

Byzantine Empire

Frankish Kingdom at accession of Charlemagne, 768

Territory conquered by Charlemagne, 768–814

Peoples dependent on Frankish rulers

Bulgars

Constantinople

THE EMPIRE

Baghdad

CALIPHATE

THE CAROLINGIAN EMPIRE

prevailing in every part of his realm, generating in the process a revival which has been given an impressive designation—the Carolingian renaissance. He who had been crowned king as "Charles" was not long in becoming "Charles the Great."

As Charlemagne strode across his realm, compelling, persuading, and guiding his subjects into new ways, some of his admirers began to sense that a millennium was at hand. A poet writing in 799 hailed him as "King Charles, head of the world and summit of Europe." In a dramatic event on Christmas Day, 800, Pope Leo III placed a crown on his head while the throng assembled in St. Peter's Church in Rome thrice acclaimed him "August Charles, crowned by God, great and peace-bringing emperor of the Romans." Whatever else this event may have meant, it was to contemporaries a suitable culmination of their hero's successes. The evocation of an ancient and glorious title in favor of a Germanic prince was symbolic of the conviction that the West had once again been incorporated into the mainstream of civilized life, represented by the splendor of ancient imperial Rome. It was Alcuin, the Anglo-Saxon scholar and trusted confidant of Charlemagne, who best summed up the conviction of the era: "Blessed is the nation over which God is the Lord. Blessed is the people exalted by a chief and sustained by a preacher of the faith whose right hand brandishes the sword of triumphant power and whose mouth makes sound the trumpet of catholic preaching. So it was when David, chosen by God as the king of the people who were then the chosen people of God . . . , subjected to Israel by his victorious sword the neighboring peoples and preached among his own people the law of

God. From the noble race of Israel there descended to save the world Christ . . . , who in our day has conceded to his chosen people as guide and teacher another king David, under the same name [the courtiers called Charlemagne "David"], animated by the same virtue and the same faith. Under his shadow the Christian people lives in peace and the pagan nations stand everywhere in terror. His devotion by its evangelical strength never ceases to fortify the catholic faith against the promoters of heresy; neither does anything new or contrary to apostolic doctrine intrude itself into any corner by secret devices. Instead by the light of celestial grace the catholic faith grows more splendid everywhere."

From Alcuin's paean emerges the clue to the nature and conformation of the historical situation at the end of the eighth century. He reflects a proud and vibrant consciousness that in the West a new society has been delineated in its geographical, institutional, spiritual, and intellectual configurations. For him the chaos, the drifting of the "dark age," has ended, and the new society has assumed the burden of sustaining civilization. A great moment in history had arrived—the Germanic masters of the West felt themselves surely and permanently in possession of the power and the grace to guide the course of civilized life. They were at once the heirs of God's first chosen people and of the splendid Romans; they had both David and Constantine to assure the progress of mankind towards its appointed destiny.

By 800 there was more than a man to serve as an external symbol of the resurgence of the West. There was a new city, often called by contemporaries the "new Jerusalem" and the "second Rome," arising in the heart of the Frankish homeland to reflect the West's abundant vigor and growing talent. This was Aix-la-Chapelle, Charlemagne's city, built just before 800 amidst the exhilarating successes enjoyed by "David," soon to be emperor of the Romans. Its creation and its activities reflect the aspirations, the talents, and the ways of the nascent Western European society in the act of establishing its place in the historical spectrum. If one can vicariously relive the life that unfolded within its confines, he may recapture the essence of "the first Europe," a society whose most glorious days lay in the future, but one which never entirely transcended its first moment of conscious existence at the end of the eighth century.

## two

## "A SECOND ROME, A NEW JERUSALEM"

Ոot the least important indication of the new vigor
of Carolingian society was the ability to build a new city
—a rare achievement in the moribund West after the fall
of Rome. We can profitably begin our search for an understanding of "the first Europe" by seeking clues to the
tastes, ideas, and skills displayed in the monuments built
in Aix during the age of Charlemagne.

The decision to build a city worthy of the "head of the
world and the summit of Europe" appears to have been
made shortly after Charlemagne spent the winter of 788–89
at the modest royal villa which had been built at Aix by the
Merovingians and inherited by the Carolingians. The precise reason for this decision escapes us. Frankish kings had
never before had a fixed capital; they moved constantly
from one villa to another in order to utilize most expe-
ditiously the produce of their scattered estates and to main-
tain the personal bonds upon which royal power depended.
Charlemagne's successes during the first quarter-century
of his reign probably made this peripatetic existence increasingly less satisfactory. More intensified administrative,
religious, and cultural activity may have created problems
which could be better handled from a fixed center. The
booty from military victories provided the means to build
a more impressive royal residence. Charlemagne may have

been thinking of a burial place befitting his growing fame; both his father and his grandfather were buried at the abbey of St. Denis near Paris, where they slumbered in the shadow of a famous saint. But the most compelling reason for building Aix was Charlemagne's increasing awareness of his singular role in the West. From all sides men hailed him in superlatives such as no Western potentate had enjoyed since the last great Christian Roman emperors. His learned advisers, steeped in theology and history, called him a second Constantine, a new David. Had not Constantine and David crowned their careers by building cities? Why not the second Constantine, the new David?

The only solid evidence indicating why Aix-la-Chapelle was chosen as the site of the new city comes from Einhard, who wrote that Charlemagne "loved the vapors of the naturally warm waters . . . and therefore constructed a royal residence at Aix-la-Chapelle." The personal predilections of the great man may indeed have been decisive. Certainly Aix had no already established fame. During the first three centuries of the Christian era it had enjoyed modest importance as a nodule in the Roman communications system supporting the frontier defenses and as a vacation spot for Roman soldiers, who likewise enjoyed the baths. Much later, after the Roman city had fallen into ruins, the Merovingians built a modest villa and chapel at Aix. The Carolingians fell heir to this villa and used it occasionally during their travels, but certainly not enough to suggest that it was a favorite villa until Charlemagne discovered the pleasures of its warm springs. No doubt this attraction was reinforced by certain geopolitical advantages offered by Aix: its location in the heart of the old Austrasian kingdom where the Carolingians had originated and where their chief aristocratic supporters lived, and its strategic proximity to the crucial Saxon area.

Historians have tended to belittle the builders of Aix by dismissing them as "imitative," a characterization that is not entirely adequate in the light of the conventions prevailing at the end of the eighth century. The new church supplies the best indication. At the very time when Aix was being planned, several impressive churches were built in the Frankish kingdom with the assistance of Charlemagne—the abbey churches of St. Denis near Paris, of St. Riquier near Abbéville, and of St. Boniface at Fulda. All were basilican structures, based on an architectural form that had originated for use in Roman public buildings and had evolved over several centuries to suit the needs of Christian worship. The ground plan of a basilica consisted of a rectangular nave flanked by side aisles. On the east a small apse, often semicircular, was added to contain the altar. As the basilican form evolved, rectangular wings were added on the north and south to serve as additional places of worship, thus constituting a transept near the eastern end of the long nave. The nave was elevated higher than the flanking aisles, creating a triforium level where the walls were pierced by windows to light the interior of the nave. Such would have been the church at Aix had Charlemagne been imitative.

The planners of a second Rome, a new Jerusalem in the West, were not content to do what was being done around them. They sought a style that would have a regal quality unique in their milieu. Yet they were realistic enough to know that they must build a city suited to the practical dictates of current economic, administrative, and religious usages. Their plans were synthesized from accepted usages and from ideas new to the Frankish world. The heart of the city was laid out on the pattern of a conventional eighth-century villa, with the lord's residence as a center around which were constructed buildings needed to house his retainers and the various functions associated with the maintenance of his household. But in their search for the means of glorifying the unique figure who would occupy Aix's royal residence, the planners became experimental. They turned to a style that had been perfected in another age and another milieu and had long since ceased to be employed in the West. They found their prototypes in Italy and the architecture of the fifth and sixth centuries. The church of S. Vitale in Ravenna was undoubtedly the chief model for the new church at Aix, and probably the palaces of Ravenna, Pavia, and Rome guided the style of the chief secular buildings. It would help to understand Carolingian mentality if we could know why the court circle chose these particular prototypes. It is not quite enough to say that admiration for classical civilization dictated the choice, for the court circle must have realized that their models were hardly "classical." More likely, Charlemagne and his confidants felt that this style would give the new court an appearance similar to the imperial court at Constantinople, which in Western eyes represented the acme of majesty. If we cannot be sure why the Carolingians turned to Italian models for inspiration, we can say with certainty that their choice made Aix a unique city in the Frankish West; this distinctiveness is probably what Charlemagne most desired.

The building of Aix was a project to test the authority

and organizational skill of Charlemagne. A late ninth-century biographer of Charlemagne, Notker, the monk of St. Gall, describes the method followed in organizing a major building project: "Now it was a custom at that time that if the imperial order was given for the accomplishment of any project, whether it was the building of bridges, ships, or causeways, or the cleaning, paving, or filling up of muddy roads, the counts might execute the less important works by the agency of their deputies or servants. But for greater enterprises, and especially those that were new works, no duke or count, no bishop or abbott could possibly get himself excused. The arches of the great bridge at Mainz bear witness to this, for all Europe, so to speak, labored at this work in orderly co-operation. . . . If any churches located on royal property needed decorating with carved ceilings or wall paintings, the neighboring bishops and abbots had to take charge of the task. But if new churches had to be built, all bishops, dukes, counts, abbots, heads of royal churches, and all who were in occupation of any public benefice had to work on it with never ceasing labor from its foundations to its roof."

In an economy lacking extensive exchange and large numbers of specialized craftsmen for hire the requisition system described by Notker served chiefly to supply material and labor. Money was not a prime concern. Einhard suggests that Charlemagne spent generously from his own treasury to build Aix. It was well filled at the moment as a result of the booty seized from the Avars between 791 and 796. One chronicler wrote that it took fifteen wagons, each pulled by four oxen, to haul to Aix the loot seized from the Avars in 795. What the King needed to build his city was stone, timbers, metal, paints, and glass. Local officials from many parts of the kingdom were ordered to procure and transport these items to Aix. Careful studies of the remains of the church indicate, for example, that the stone came from several areas of the empire. Distance was no obstacle when something was needed to provide an extra touch of elegance. Einhard wrote that "since Charles could not obtain columns elsewhere for building [the church], he had them brought from Rome and Ravenna." A surviving papal letter indicates that the King took personal charge of such matters; he wrote to Pope Hadrian I asking permission to remove "mosaics, marbles, and certain other items both in the floor and the walls of the palace of the city of Ravenna."

Skilled labor was also imported to construct the city. Many laborers came from the dependent population of royal estates. One of the most celebrated documents of the age, a royal directive called the *Capitulare de villis* issued to guide the management of royal estates, stressed the importance of maintaining a full complement of artisans on each estate. Charlemagne also required his officials and vassals to send artisans from their estates to work at Aix. However, not all the laborers who built Aix were serfs. Notker speaks of a brass worker at Aix who was a monk from St. Gall, indicating that Charlemagne tapped the considerable talent of the monasteries of his realm for skilled artisans. Notker also says that the King recruited artisans "from overseas," which may mean Italy, England, Ireland, or even the East. These must have been laborers working for hire. Probably the vast project attracted workmen to Aix. The *Royal Annals of the Franks* recounts that when Emperor Louis was at Ingelheim in 826, "there came . . . a certain priest Georgius from Venice, who claimed that he could build an organ; the emperor sent him to Aix-la-Chapelle with the treasurer Thanculfus and ordered the latter to provide all that was necessary for building the instrument." Thus the work force which built Aix constituted a varied collection of serfs and freemen, priests and peasants, monks and professional artisans, local residents and foreigners.

A court poet, whose effort suffers in translation, paints this picture of the bustle surrounding the building of the city: "Here a second Rome, a new flower, grand and extraordinary, raises its high walls, its wonderfully splendid towers until they almost touch the stars. There stands the pious Charles on an elevated place, giving signals and disposing the high walls of the future Rome. Here he orders a forum and there a sacred senate to be placed. . . . Crowds of workmen move about. Some cut suitable stones into round columns and put high arches in place. And others struggle with their hands to roll stones into place. Some build a gateway, while others lay the deep foundations of a theater and enclose an atrium with soaring vaults. Still others labor to capture the warm waters."

We may be sure that whenever he was present, the tireless King concerned himself with the progress of his workmen. Probably the chief supervision was provided by court officials empowered by the King to direct the building. Perhaps certain individuals were charged with general supervisory powers, while others directed specific aspects of the work. For example, two individuals, an abbot and a court steward, are mentioned as supervisers of workmen;

their duties included providing food, clothing, and materials as well as direction for the laborers. The construction seems to have progressed with a minimum of difficulty, although there were occasional problems. Notker tells of one knavish abbot who grew rich by allowing workers willing to pay him to go home while forcing those remaining to do the work. Another official profited by stinting the workmen he was supposed to feed and clothe. An artisan commissioned to make a bell was detected using inferior materials. There was apparently some grumbling among the magnates forced to supply laborers and material; one bishop wrote rather heatedly to a court official insisting that he could not afford to furnish any more assistance to royal building activities. On the whole, however, these were exceptions. Although new additions were made during Charlemagne's last years and throughout Louis' reign, the construction of the new city moved forward rapidly enough that Charlemagne and a large retinue could spend nearly every winter after 794 at the new residence. This rapidity mirrors the discipline, order, and organization which the great Carolingians were able to impose on their subjects.

What emerged from this enterprise at which "all of Europe, so to speak, labored"? The heart of the new city was a complex of buildings usually called the *palatium*. The ravages of time make a complete reconstruction impossible, but its general features are evident. The *palatium* occupied the sector of modern Aachen where the city hall and the cathedral are located. The perimeter of this area may have been enclosed by a wall with gates giving access to the interior or simply guarded by individual watch towers from which traffic could be surveyed. The enclosure was essentially the living area of the ruler and his entourage, a glorified royal country estate where every aspect of the business of managing the royal household and the lord's realm could be conducted.

Within the enclosure the new church, built in honor of Our Lady, was certainly the most imposing and unique structure, an impressive reflection of the powerful religious convictions and the sophisticated tastes of the royal court. Recent archaeological explorations indicate that it was built over the altar of an earlier chapel which housed important relics. The structure was about 160 feet long and 115 feet wide, representing a building of major proportions, especially when compared to the modest chapel it replaced.

There were, however, larger churches in the Carolingian realm. What was more striking was the unique design of the new structure, clearly apparent from its external appearance. Instead of the conventional basilican structure with its plain, rectangular nave, transept, and apse, the church was composed of three connected but distinct structures. The first was a sixteen-sided central structure rising two stories high and crowned by an octagonal drum of roughly half the diameter of the lower part. The roof of the upper octagon reached almost 110 feet above the ground. The second part consisted of a small two-story apse attached to the east side of the central structure. Finally, on the west was appended an imposing entrance structure rising three stories high and flanked on either side by towers semicircular in plan which merged into the entrance structure. The outside of the church was relatively unadorned except for an attractive cornice topping the walls of the rotunda, mouldings around the entrance structure and the upper octagon, and pilasters with a strong classical flavor framing each window of the upper drum. All the windows of the church were strongly articulated by finished stone casements contrasting with the rough-hewn, heavily cemented masonry of the external walls. In its entirety the exterior of the church conveyed a sense of primitive simplicity, vigor, and strength.

The west entrance to the church was guarded by a forecourt or atrium measuring about 100 feet long and 58 feet wide. The atrium was surrounded on the north, west, and south by an arcade in two tiers. On the ground level the arcade opened directly into the forecourt, each of the arches framed by graceful columns with a strong classical cast. In the center of the atrium was a fountain adorned by a bronze bear from whose breast water flowed. The whole atrium was dominated by the sober west façade and its flanking towers. The façade bears a strong resemblance to a Roman triumphal arch into which has been set a large arched niche pierced at the ground level by the main entrance door, a small square window above it, and then still higher up a larger window framed by a round arch. The exact appearance of the façade above the niche is not clear, since later changes were made which removed the original structure. Almost certainly the whole atrium complex served ceremonial purposes. Perhaps it was used as a gathering place for the veneration of relics displayed from inside the church through the small square window in the façade. One can imagine that upon entering this cloister-like area the faithful began to sense the atmosphere of piety and holiness befitting a great shrine; perhaps a quiet prevailed here which contrasted sharply with the bustle elsewhere in the palace complex.

42

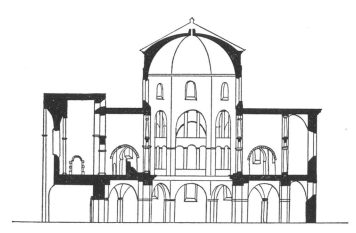

*Cross Section*

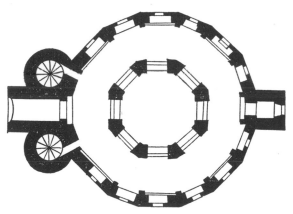

*Floor Plan*

CHARLEMAGNE'S CHURCH AT AIX-LA-CHAPELLE

The great bronze entrance doors with their handles shaped like lions' heads led through a barrel-vaulted passageway or narthex into the church proper. The main chamber of the church consisted of an inner octagonal rotunda about 54 feet across completely surrounded by vaulted aisles on two levels, the first at the ground level and the second at the triforium level. The rotunda was constructed so that it constituted a chamber with its own unity and character. At the ground level the eight points of the octagon were marked by sturdy pillars spanned by eight massive round arches. These pillars and arches supported a second tier of eight more pillars, not quite so heavy but somewhat taller, which also culminated in round arches. Each opening between the pillars at the triforium level was divided into three smaller openings by an interesting arrangement of polished stone columns. Four columns were employed for each opening. Two rested on bases placed at the level of the triforium and reached about halfway up the opening. Above their Corinthian capitals they were linked together and to the flanking main pillars by small arches which supported a ledge. On this ledge were placed two more columns reaching to the arch spanning the main pillars. Above the triforium, radiating light into the rotunda over the roof of the ambulatory, was a clerestory. Each wall of the octagon at this level was pierced by a round-arched window. Finally, the octagon was covered by a well-fashioned stone dome. Its construction, requiring that eight surfaces be curved upward and inward to a central point, may have been the chief test of the builders' skill. The keystone of the dome was about 104 feet above the floor of the octagon. In the rotunda the architect achieved an interesting effect.

44

The progression from large openings at the ground level to smaller ones at the triforium level to still smaller ones at the clerestory level is aesthetically pleasing. The skillful positioning of pillars, arches, and columns creates the impression that the main octagon is an enclosed chamber, a kind of inner sanctum opening upward toward the dome of heaven symbolically represented by the actual dome covering the rotunda.

The aisles encircling the central octagon at the ground and triforium levels confronted the builders with complex technical problems. Their inner boundaries were marked by the eight pillars of the rotunda, while the outer wall had sixteen sides. This arrangement posed a complex vaulting problem which was mastered in a way that demonstrates the high degree of technical competence of the builders. Windows pierced each of the sixteen segments of the thick external walls except the one covered by the apse on the east and the three covered by the façade structure on the west. The aisle at the triforium level, which could be reached only by spiral stairways in each of the towers flanking the main entrance, had a more elegant appearance than the lower one, as was fitting for the part of the church closer to God and reserved for the use of the rulers of Aix. Especially graceful were the polished porphyry columns set between the main pillars and the breast-high bronze fences, each designed differently, used to guard the openings into the central octagon. The aisles at both levels may have served as places to locate subsidiary altars installed to serve the needs of the numerous clergy attached to the court. At least on the ground floor, wooden stalls may have been placed in the openings between the rotunda pillars. The two chief altars of the church—one honoring the Virgin on the first floor and one dedicated to the Savior on the second —almost certainly stood in the ambulatories on the east just before the passageway into the apse.

It is difficult to know exactly what the original Carolingian apse looked like, since it was replaced in the fourteenth century by the present Gothic choir. Recent excavations exposing the foundations of the Carolingian apse show that it was a modest structure, roughly as wide as the passageway between the two main pillars on the eastern side of the octagon—about seventeen feet—and about sixteen feet deep. There were probably windows in the east side of the apse at each level. As already noted, a major altar was placed in the ambulatory before the opening leading into the apse at each level. The chamber of the lower story of the apse may have been occupied by a cathedra set against the eastern wall for the use of high-ranking clergymen assisting at mass. The upper chamber probably served as a repository for an important relic.

The second and third levels of the west façade of the church contained chambers reached by the circular stairways in each tower flanking that part of the building. The chamber on the second floor directly above the entrance passage has been named the "Emperor's Loge" by modern authorities. Its purpose has aroused considerable speculation, but almost certainly it served as a chapel, perhaps so placed to guard the church from evil spirits from the west or to convey the idea that God is everywhere. The altar in this chapel was probably located against the western wall directly in front of the small square window already noted in our description of the external appearance of the façade.

Because of its location low in the western wall and because of its shape, it seems that this window could only have served to display relics or insignia so that they could be seen from the atrium. Higher up was a larger window providing the main source of light for the Emperor's Loge. On the east, a large arched opening, divided into three small passageways by double tiers of polished columns, led into the triforium ambulatory. The space in the ambulatory just outside the Emperor's Loge was a special one, for here stood the throne from which the Emperor assisted at mass. The throne, which may have been modeled after that of Solomon described in the Book of Kings, consisted of a stone seat placed on a platform raised six steps above the floor. It faced eastward across the main octagon toward the apse before which stood the altar of the Savior. Almost nothing is known about the chamber on the story above the Emperor's Loge, since the original structure has been radically changed.

We have already noted that access to the second and third levels of the church was gained by climbing stairs in either of the towers; entrance to these stairs was gained by doorways leading from the lower ambulatory on either side of the main entrance. However, there was another way to reach the Emperor's Loge. A door cut through the west side of the north tower at the second level led to a two-storied covered passageway which reached from the church to the royal residence hall. This arrangement permitted the ruler and his entourage to go from the throne through the Emperor's Loge directly to the royal living quarters without going outside or descending to the ground level.

The new church's decor was probably as impressive to

contemporaries as its unique architectural features. Although numerous changes over the centuries have obliterated almost all the original ornamentation, one can from literary sources and from inferences based on survivals of Carolingian art elsewhere form a general idea of the objects, themes, and techniques employed to adorn the church. From these sources it is clear that several different aesthetic considerations influenced the decoration of the church. The Carolingians were not so far removed from their Germanic heritage as to have outgrown the barbaric taste for the glitter of precious metal and jewels and for the complex symmetry of geometric designs. At the same time, they were heirs to a living tradition of Christian art comprised chiefly of pregnant symbols suggesting the essential meaning of the faith. Charlemagne's court had only recently fallen under the sway of "classical" art and was eager to use it. Finally, important theological considerations were posed at the very moment the church was being built. As a result of his involvement in the iconoclastic struggle, Charlemagne was forced to take a position on the proper use of images in church decoration. In a polemical tract called the *Caroline Books,* composed to correct Byzantine errors, Charlemagne's court posited this general principle with respect to church decoration: "While we spurn everything in the way of adoration of images, indeed we permit all to have the images of saints in basilicas not for adoration but as reminders of their deeds and adornments for the walls." Essentially this amounted to a restatement of a position once taken by Pope Gregory I: "Painting is admissible in churches in order that those who cannot read may yet read by seeing on the walls what they cannot read in books."

Art was essentially the Bible of the ignorant, a teaching device serving simultaneously a decorative function.

The Germanic love for ornateness and the prevailing modes in church furnishings were especially evident in the lustrous collection of movable articles provided for use in the conduct of divine services. Altars, chalices, reliquaries, liturgical books, candelabra, and vestments of many varieties and great richness lent an atmosphere of splendor to the church. Little survives from the actual Carolingian furnishings of the church at Aix, but from such items from other Carolingian churches and from many dedicatory verses written to celebrate the addition of these items to the church's collection, one cannot miss the taste for lavishness. The dedicatory verses suggest that Carolingian society not only enjoyed the glitter and richness but also felt that God was equally pleased. One suspects that it was this kind of decor that appealed most to Charlemagne. Einhard confines his description of his hero's contribution to the beautification of the church to these remarks: "He adorned the church with gold and silver, with lamps, and with solid brass railings and doors. . . . He provided gold and silver vessels and priestly vestments in such great quantities that at religious ceremonies not even the doorkeepers, who are the lowest ecclesiastical order, could perform their duties in their usual garments." The King's efforts were complemented by a flood of gifts from Rome, Constantinople, Baghdad, Jerusalem, Spain, and every corner of the Frankish realm. Among them was an organ sent by Emperor Constantine V which made "the sound of thunder through its power, and at the same time had the sweetness of a lyre or cymbal." Surely few churches in the West surpassed

49

Aix for the richness, variety, and splendor of its furnishings.

Only meager sources inform us of the new church's paintings and mosaics, but it appears that they were dominated by a sober didactic spirit. A twelfth-century writer said that Charlemagne "ordered that the church be painted with stories from the Old and New Testaments." Certainly this would have been in keeping with prevailing usages, as is evident, for example, in the frescoes of the abbey church at Mustair in Switzerland with its eighty scenes centered on the Last Judgment. The sort of theme the court preferred is suggested by a passage in Ermoldus Nigellus' *Poem in Honor of Emperor Louis* describing the paintings in the church built at Ingelheim by Charlemagne and Louis. Ermoldus says that on the left side of this church were paintings representing episodes in Old Testament history, while on the right were paintings "of the mortal deeds of Christ." Carolingian poetry suggests that episodes from the life of Christ provided themes for large-scale decorative compositions. We can be virtually certain that the church at Aix contained frescoes telling biblical stories. The number and location of these paintings is not clear. The unusual shape of the church did not provide the ample wall spaces available in a basilican church for vast narrative cycles. The most likely areas for scriptural scenes at Aix were the clerestory, the Emperor's Loge, and the apses.

A ninth-century poet's remark that he saw at Aix a "golden representation . . . at the top of the columns" indicates that a mosaic adorned the dome of the new church. A seventeenth-century sketch purports to reproduce part of the Carolingian mosiac; it was a model for the restoration now seen at Aachen. The sketch portrays the three eastern segments of the dome. Christ sits enthroned in the central panel, his shoulders draped with a purple mantle and his right hand raised in a blessing. Two angels hover over him on either side in a golden, star-filled heaven. Behind the throne is a representation of a globe. Below Christ are the figures of seven of the twenty-four elders of the Apocalypse; the remainder must have been portrayed on the other segments of the dome. Each elder is represented in a different posture as he rises to offer his crown to Christ, lending a dynamic quality to the composition which contrasts with the stiff majesty of Christ. Literary sources confirm that the theme of Christ in majesty was popular among the Carolingians; a poem by Alcuin depicting Charlemagne praying before such a composition may well be a description of the dome mosaic at Aix. A surviving Carolingian mosiac in the church at Germigny-des-Prés, built by the court favorite Theodulf, supplies an example of Carolingian skill in mosaic work.

Aside from the pictorial art of the frescoes and mosaics, the church at Aix was undoubtedly adorned by a prolific use of painted and mosaic designs on pillars, arches, window frames, vaults, capitals, cornices, and any part of a wall that offered a blank space. From surviving manuscript decorations it appears that these decorative designs mixed together Germanic geometric patterns with classical floral and architectural figures to create a colorful synthesis. The floors were covered with contrasting tiles set in geometric patterns. There was probably little large-scale sculpture in the church, unless some was brought from Italy, for the Carolingians seem to have been uninterested in or incapable of executing three-dimensional sculpture of large proportions. They did execute carved relief work for decorative purposes.

Probably the most significant art work contained in the new church was the painted manuscript illuminations in the various liturgical books and the ivory carvings used for book covers and altar diptychs. In these two media Carolingian artists demonstrated some of their best talent and conducted some of their most fruitful artistic experimentation. Carolingian miniaturists and ivory carvers worked from a long and complex tradition involving late classical, primitive Christian, Byzantine, Syrian, Irish, Anglo-Saxon, and Merovingian models. A study of their products is further complicated by the several schools of illuminators and ivory carvers which flourished in Charlemagne's realm. The church at Aix undoubtedly possessed a collection illustrating these diverse traditions and representing the various workshops of the empire. Some of the books and ivories were produced in the palace workshop organized and patronized by the King. Others came from monastic scriptoria and ateliers scattered around the empire, for nothing pleased the rulers more than to receive a fine book as a gift and few triumphs were sweeter for a provincial workshop than to produce a book that would please the court. There were also books and ivories of foreign origin at Aix—from England, Ireland, Italy, and even the East.

Carolingian miniature paintings and ivory carvings were closely circumscribed by close ties to the liturgy and by a narrow group of subjects within the religious framework. Illuminations were confined chiefly to gospel books, Bibles, psalters, and sacramentaries, while the ivory carvers worked almost exclusively on book covers and altar diptychs. An occasional portrait of the evangelists or of David, portrayals of the fountain of life, the adoration of the lamb, or Christ in majesty, and a few narrative scenes depicting biblical episodes composed almost the total range of pictorial subjects. Divisions of liturgical texts were often marked by highly ornate capital letters, while individual pages were usually framed with elaborate decorative designs.

As decorators the Carolingian artists achieved an amazing richness of design and coloring, an almost barbarian luxuriousness. The opulence of the illuminated manuscripts defies easy description. One must, for example, see for himself the Godescalc gospel book, made on Charlemagne's order for himself and his wife, to appreciate the effect achieved by the use of gold letter on purple vellum. Nor can one convey verbally the luxurious, almost jewel-like effect achieved by the use of rich colors in the intricate floral and geometric designs which constituted the full-page capital letters used to divide sections of psalters and Bibles. Especially impressive as pure decoration were the ornamental frameworks used to surround the columns of a written text. A close study of these frameworks reveals an amazing repertory of decorative motifs—flowers, plants, animals, geometric patterns, knots, interlaces, columns, arches, scrolls, and even stylized human figures—mingled together with infinite care to create striking effects. Carolingian decorative art showed strong Germanic and Celtic influences; however, artists enriched these traditions by adding classical and oriental decorative themes. Some of the motifs recaptured from the classical tradition were destined to exert a decisive influence on Western European art.

After a contemporary viewer had finished admiring the

decorative richness of the manuscripts, he may have sensed a quality in the paintings and ivory carvings that was unfamiliar to his conventional tastes. If one surveys pre-Carolingian illumination in the West, he feels that artists were slowly forgetting the art of illustration in favor of pure decoration. He senses that part of the barbarization of the West in the "dark age" involved the emptying of life from art in favor of design and color, the draining away of the substance of plants, animals, and human figures in the search for decorative effect. The Carolingian artists reversed this pattern by reinserting in their works a dramatic, narrative element. This return to narrative art was beyond question the chief development of the age of Charlemagne. Chiefly in late classical, Byzantine, and Syrian prototypes they found models for the portraits, the biblical narratives, and the mythological themes which they used for didactic purposes in the art of the illuminated manuscript and in ivory carving. Although the typical Carolingian artist managed to reconcile the urge to decorate and the urge to illustrate and teach, there was a tendency in maturing Carolingian art for the narrative, illustrative, didactic element to grow more important. Occasionally this latter element took over completely, as in the Utrecht Psalter. The 160 pen and ink sketches in this masterpiece have little decorative value, but the energetic scenes crowded with tiny human figures succeed remarkably well in summarizing the themes of the psalms, in letting one read without reading.

The enrichment of the motifs and subjects at their disposal put new technical demands on the Carolingian miniaturists and ivory carvers. They demonstrated increasing skill and inventiveness in design, composition, and use of color. Some problems still baffled them, including especially perspective and three-dimensional effects. On the whole, however, they managed to recover many techniques nearly abandoned in the West and to learn how to use them with discipline and taste. As one views a representative collection of Carolingian manuscripts and ivories, he senses that in the tiny scenes before him much of the history of Western European pictorial art is prefigured.

Viewed as a whole, the decoration of the church at Aix represented a remarkable synthesis of Germanic, Celtic, and Mediterranean elements. Especially noteworthy was the greater prominence given to Mediterranean themes and techniques than was usual in the Germanic world. This archaizing tendency was inspired not so much by aesthetic considerations as by an urge to discover in the past more effective ways of conveying religious truths. Carolingian artists and their patrons were not so much slavish imitators as they were conscious seekers for a wider range of models by which they could express more eloquently and intelligently their increasingly sophisticated ideas and more subtle emotions. The importance of the court artists who built and decorated the church at Aix lay in the fact that they possessed the mandate and the resources to search for artistic concepts in the past more thoroughly and more systematically than did artists working elsewhere in the West. Their enriched experience was soon transplanted to other centers of artistic activity. The church at Aix thus served as a combined atelier and museum, helping to fix an art style that can properly be called "Carolingian," one which marked a significant step in the artistic evolution of Western Europe. Those who visited the church at Aix in the age of Charlemagne were witnesses to an important event in art history, one compounded out of the vigorous Germanic spirit seeking to enrich itself from the tradition of antiquity so that it could better honor God.

The counterpart of the splendid new church was the royal hall built up a slope roughly three hundred feet to the north. Unfortunately, all but a few remnants of its walls and foundations have disappeared, making its reconstruction an uncertain task. The royal hall was seemingly a plain, two-story, rectangular structure built of stone, with its long axis lying east and west. Perhaps a square tower was raised above the main structure, for a later witness spoke of seeing the structure's shining roof, on top of which was a bronze eagle with spread wings, as he approached the city of Aix. The main entrance of the royal hall faced south toward the church. Some authorities have surmised that this entrance was given a monumental quality by the addition of a porch, a balcony, and a stairway, all modeled after palaces in Italy.

The second story of the royal hall apparently consisted of a huge reception room where public business was conducted and banquets held. This room was made more impressive by the addition of a semicircular bay on the west which provided the setting for the royal throne used by the king when he presided over assemblages gathered there. Probably the hall was lighted by windows similar to those in the church and heated by great open fireplaces along the walls. Apparently the ceiling was timbered, for it is doubtful that Carolingian builders would have attempted to build a stone vault almost one hundred feet long to span the seventy feet separating the side walls. Below the reception hall were ground-floor chambers created by the thick transverse walls constructed to support the floor of the reception hall. These chambers served the domestic needs of the royal household; here were kitchens, store-rooms, workshops, and domestic quarters. For, in building their new palace, the Carolingians could not overlook a basic reality of the age—the King's household depended absolutely on its own resources. The precise location and disposition of the royal living quarters is not clear. Various sources mention Charlemagne's bed chamber and an ante-room outside it where his various officials awaited his appearance each morning. Notker records that the royal living quarters gave access to a "solarium" or terrace guarded by a balustrade from which the King could look out over the palace enclosure and see what was going on. This suggests that the King and his large family had quarters on the second floor; probably the personal servants of the royal family were housed on the first floor of the royal hall.

As in the case of the church, the decor of the royal residence reflected the florid tastes of the age mingled with the didactic urge. A twelfth-century source says that the great reception hall contained paintings depicting Charlemagne's Spanish wars and the seven liberal arts. From the poet Ermoldus Nigellus we have a detailed description of the historical scenes decorating the royal hall at Ingelheim. On one side were scenes portraying the deeds of ancient kings and heroes. On the other were representatives of more recent events—the founding of Constantinople, the deeds of Theodoric, Charles Martel's conquest of Frisia, Pepin's wars in Aquitaine, and Charlemagne's victories in Saxony. This treatment was obviously intended to place the Carolingians in the tradition of greatness, and it would seem logical to think that a comparable effort would have been made in the decoration of the palace at Aix. Carolingian poetry and miniatures indicate that artists portrayed the liberal arts by personifying each art and often the virtues associated with each. This manner of symbolizing the liberal arts was undoubtedly borrowed from the classical tradition. In addition to its paintings, the royal hall was made resplendent by those objects of gold, silver, and jewels which so pleased the Germanic tastes of the court circle. Einhard's description of the treasure left by Charlemagne gives some indication of the objects which graced the royal hall. A few especially impressive items were probably prominently displayed: a rectangular silver table depicting the city of Constantinople, a round silver table showing Rome, and a third silver table, "more beautiful in workmanship and much greater in weight than the others," adorned with a map of the world. Rich  tapestries, ornate candelabra, the prizes of many wars and hunting expeditions, and carved wooden furniture undoubtedly graced the main halls and combined with expensive serving vessels to establish an atmosphere of opulent splendor. Many of these items were gifts from distant lands, while others were fabricated by royal artisans living in the palace.

The open space between the royal hall and the church constituted a large courtyard used for the numerous activities associated with the regular business of the court. In its center stood an equestrian statue of Theodoric the Ostrogoth brought to Aix from Italy by Charlemagne. The courtyard was virtually enclosed by other buildings making up the *palatium*. On the west was the already mentioned two-story porticus, over three hundred feet long, serving as a covered passage linking the royal residence and the church. Some literary sources suggest that on the side of the gallery facing into the courtyard there was a covered arcade, where guards, retainers, and loiterers could find protection from the weather. Otherwise, we know virtually nothing of the disposition of the main buildings making up the *palatium* complex. None was more famed than the bath, which, according to Einhard, was so large that Charlemagne "invited not only his sons, but also his nobles and friends, and even his dependents and bodyguards to the bath, so that not seldom there were a hundred or more men bathing at once." There was certainly a chapter house for the palace clergy, as suggested by Einhard's statement that just before Charlemagne's death a bolt of lightning "knocked off the golden apple which decorated the top of the roof of the church, and hurled it on the roof of the house of the priests which was next to the church." The extensive educational activity of the court may have required a special building for classrooms, a scriptorium, and a library. Other sources hint at the existence of a treasure house, a mint, a hostel for pilgrimages, workshops, and storehouses located near the royal residence. There were even private residences close to the royal hall; Notker wrote that "houses of various dignitaries were, by Charles' device, built around his royal hall in such a way that from the windows of his chamber he could see all who came and went and what they were doing, although they thought they were unobserved." Attached to these houses were arcades providing loiterers with protection "from the rain and snow, from the cold and the heat."

Adjoining the *palatium* was a park, probably lying north of the royal hall. Ermoldus Nigellus describes it as follows: "There was a small area near the famed royal palace at Aix enclosed by a solid stone wall, planted with trees, and covered with green grass. A small river flowed slowly through it. The park was filled with birds and savage beasts. When the King was so inclined, he went there with a few companions to shoot with arrows the great horned stags, to strike down the bucks and does, or when the winter's ice hardened the earth, to pursue birds with the falcons." A court confidant and poet, Angilbert, provides a similar description, adding that the stream had many fish. In another poem he speaks of the royal children playing in the park in terms that suggest that there may have been a formal garden close to the royal hall.

Perhaps during the first years of Charlemagne's residence in Aix the city consisted of little more than the *palatium*. Soon, however, a "city" in a larger sense emerged. A cemetery was built, and Charlemagne provided a well. A legal document of the ninth century mentions a church in Aix dedicated to St. Martin. Residences were constructed by lay and ecclesiastical magnates, probably at the encouragement of Charlemagne, who according to one source "took care insofar as possible to draw officials . . . from the diverse regions [of his kingdom] in order to provide easier access to the palace to all subjects who would thus be sure that they would meet members of their family or acquaintances from their regions at the palace." The magnates appear to have built sizable establishments. For example, the residences of Einhard and the archchaplain Hilduin both had private chapels; Einhard's chapel was large enough to accommodate considerable crowds who came to see the bones of Saints Marcellinus and Peter which Einhard brought to Aix in 828. The great magnates apparently tried to elevate their status by surrounding themselves with a large number of retainers, thus necessitating commodious quarters but also creating a disciplinary problem serious enough to cause the King to issue orders that each noble must take steps to control his retainers and to send away those who were not absolutely needed.

Merchants soon gathered at Aix to take advantage of the demands of the court and the noble householders for luxury items. Some were transients, transacting their business in the streets of the city. A royal order of 828 granted protection to the merchants who served the palace faithfully, indicating that they had access not only to the city but also to the palace. Other merchants established permanent quarters in Aix, for a royal order empowered a royal official to conduct an investigation of "the houses of the merchants . . . both Christians and Jews" to search out undesirable persons residing there. The merchant's role in Aix was, however, a relatively narrow one, since the economy of the age dictated that even those dwelling in cities had to draw their sustenance from the produce of their rural estates. Charlemagne's edict, the *Capitulare de villis,* describes in great detail the management of a royal estate so that the court would be properly supplied with the food and handicraft products it needed. Each noble living at Aix likewise drew his sustenance from his own estates. In a letter to his chief agent, Einhard indicated the kind of preparations an important man needed to make before going to Aix: "We wish you to send certain men to Aix who will prepare our house and replenish all which is needed for us to live there, that is, flour, beer, wine, cheese, and so forth." A common sight in Aix was certainly the regular appearance of wagon caravans bringing supplies for the sustenance of city households. The bulk of the city's population consisted of those who served the needs of these households.

This then was the city raised to glorify the Carolingians and proclaim their successes. Certainly it was not a large city. Probably at some seasons when the King was absent it was almost dead. Nor was its season of fame long. Perhaps it had begun to decline before the end of Louis' reign in 840, for he seemed to prefer Ingelheim as a royal residence. Near the end of the ninth century Aix was seized by the Vikings, who stabled their horses in the palace, burned the bath, and pillaged the city. Yet viewed from the perspective of early ninth-century Western Europe, the physical appearance of Aix must have conveyed another impression. The poets and scholars who compared it to Rome, Jerusalem, Athens, and Carthage were without doubt impressed by what had been built amidst the hills and forests far from the great cities of antiquity. One can imagine that the many strangers who came to Aix between 790 and 840—the primitive Saxons, the supercilious Greeks, the sophisticated Moslems from Cordova and Baghdad, the proud Romans, and the rustic Frankish nobles—each in his own way was surprised and impressed at what had been achieved in a few years. In its own setting and context the appearance of Aix spoke eloquently of the vigor, power, intelligence, and resourcefulness of the Carolingians and their subjects who collaborated to build a new city.

## "A Second Rome, a New Jerusalem"

In spite of its impressive appearance in its own milieu, Aix was still a city of a unique kind. It lacked many things we expect in a great city: a large population, factories, bustling commercial enterprises, a vigorous *bourgeoisie*, a mass labor force, competing social organizations, and great organs of communication. The entire physical outlay of the city was dictated by the interests of the King and his selected associates. As one studies the city, he is repeatedly struck by how much it was built as a rallying point for an elite who felt an urge to pool their talents for an offensive against the problems of the age, how much it was a kind of fortress sheltering a select few who felt inspired to join their talents for a great enterprise. This aspect of Aix as a center of civilization becomes even more obvious when we consider the kinds of activity which dominated it.

## thRee

## THE KING'S "HOME"

Єinhard called Aix "the home" of the King. He meant that during the winter months of nearly every year after 794 the city provided a place of partial withdrawal for the King and his retinue from the burdens attached to governing the vast kingdom into an environment where the most fundamental relationships of society found expression. His terminology invites us to pass over for the moment the dramatic affairs of state centering in Aix to consider the social life of the court during the season of royal residence. Perhaps this aspect of Aix's history will provide insight into the structure of Carolingian society, the habits of its leading actors, and the mentality governing its operation.

If we take Charlemagne's Aix as a microcosm of the Carolingian world, we must conclude that the decisive force governing that society was the personality of strong individuals. In contrast to modern society, where the individual's intellect and emotions are dominated by such abstract entities as the nation, the corporation, the profession, and the status group, the social order in Aix was shaped by a man. His personal qualities, deeds, physical appearance, gestures, words, and habits combined to elicit loyalty and obedience from men who responded to no other major allegiance. This elemental aspect of Carolingian society reminds us how little removed it was from its Germanic source and how much it was based on tribal ties that had been expanded to embrace an extensive kingdom and a diverse population.

The crucial features of Charlemagne's personality are not easy to condense into a single formula. His greatest admirers, steeped in classical literature and Christian patrology, loved to ascribe to him all the qualities stressed by the Stoics and the church fathers as befitting a king. Their efforts are seldom convincing, for Charlemagne was neither a Stoic nor a saint. On occasion he could be terrible in a barbaric fashion. For example, in 782 he vented his wrath on the rebellious Saxons by slaughtering 4,500 of them to retaliate for their treacherous murder of some of his military commanders. This was the kind of act which prompted Notker to write that the King had the power to make "the hearts of both Franks and barbarians sink" and led a court poet to say that the fear of his personal severity made all men as gentle as lambs. Usually, however, Charlemagne was mild and humane, essentially an amiable, egregious, warm-spirited man who captivated people and who was attracted to others. His fundamental character emerges most clearly in his responses to certain basic social situations.

Charlemagne's first allegiance went to his blood kinsmen. His relationship to his family illustrates how primordial the family tie was to the social order in the Frankish realm. When Aix became the royal residence, the King was the head of a large family, the offspring of several wives and mistresses. A youthful liaison with a certain Himultrud produced his oldest son, Pepin the Hunchback. In 770 Charlemagne was married to a Lombard princess as a consequence of a political alliance arranged by his mother, but the unfortunate princess was soon sent back to her father amidst the growing hostility that led to the Frankish conquest of the Lombards in 774. Charlemagne immediately married a thirteen-year-old Swabian princess, Hildegard, hailed by one author as "the mother of kings" in honor of the nine children she bore before her death in 783. Six of these children grew to adulthood—three sons, Charles, Louis, and a second Pepin (originally named Carlomann), and three daughters, Rotrud, Berta, and Gisela.

The next queen was a Frankish lady, Fastrada, who bore two daughters, Theodrada and Hiltrud, before her death in 794. When Charlemagne began to reside in Aix in 794, he was unmarried but was enjoying the favors of an Alemannian noble lady, Liutgard. Sometime between 796 and 799 this union was sanctioned by a formal marriage, which ended with the widely lamented death of Liutgard in 800. She was the King's last legal wife, but not the last woman in his life. Einhard wrote that "after her death, he had three concubines: Gersuinda of Saxon origin, who bore a daughter named Adaltrud; and Regina, who gave birth to Drogo and Hugo; and Adalinda, from whom came Theodoric." The same writer speaks of a daughter named Ruodada "from a certain concubine whose name does not now come to mind." Another source records a mistress named Magelgarda. Einhard's unabashed inclusion of the names of these concubines in his eulogistic biography suggests that each held an honorable place in the family circle, that no special stigma was attached to the absence of ecclesiastical sanction for their relationship with the King. Carolingian marriage customs still bore a strong Germanic mark, which

66

dictated that no household was complete without a female head whose position as consort made her a "wife" irrespective of sacramental consecration.

Like a proper Germanic family head, Charlemagne viewed his women chiefly as bearers of royal children and mistresses of the royal household. Only an occasional hint suggests that they played a role in political life. Einhard accused Fastrada of "turning the King from his natural kindness and accustomed mildness by her cruelty" to such an extent that two conspiracies against the King occurred while she was queen. Alcuin spoke of "joining to himself a helper, Liutgard," in his effort to secure a royal favor. Although not usually involved in politics, the royal women were vital figures in court life. They aided substantially in the management of the royal household. In a tract entitled *On the Administration of the Palace*, Archbishop Hincmar of Rheims wrote this: "The management of the palace, and especially the royal decor and the annual gifts of the vassals—except drink, food, and horses—pertained to the Queen and to the treasurer who was under her orders." This arrangement, he added, freed the King from all concern with matters pertaining to the household. One of Charlemagne's laws specifically ordered that officials charged with managing royal estates obey the Queen. Liutgard was characterized as a patroness of the arts and "sweet in words," suggesting that queens were not always relegated to the nursery and the kitchen. There is every reason to believe that Charlemagne's women were respected and needed members of the crucial family circle upon which the social structure was reared. Perhaps this explains Charlemagne's anxious letter written to Fastrada in 791 during his campaign against the Avars showing a husbandly concern for the Queen's delicate health.

The fruit of these marriages and liaisons was the numerous brood of children, ranging from the hunchbacked Pepin, born about 770, to the infants sired during Charlemagne's declining days nearly forty years later. Their welfare was always uppermost in their father's mind and their upbringing was his greatest joy. Einhard wrote that the King took care that "both his sons and his daughters were educated in the liberal studies. . . . When his sons reached that age at which it was the custom of the Franks to ride, he made them exercise themselves in arms and hunting. And he ordered that his daughters practice knitting and occupy themselves with the spinning wheel and spindle, so that they would not grow lazy; and he commanded them to be taught every good habit. . . . He was so much concerned with the education of his sons and daughters that when he was at home he never dined without them, nor did he ever go on a journey without them."

In reality, Charlemagne was not able to keep his family always with him. When Aix became the chief royal residence, Pepin the Hunchback was a prisoner, paying the penalty for his involvement in a plot against his father in 792. In 781, when they were three and four years old, Louis and the younger Pepin were sent as titular kings to the subkingdoms of Aquitaine and Italy, created to mollify the separatist sentiments in these areas. Both returned occasionally to court for brief sojourns. Undoubtedly their father viewed with pride their advance to manhood and dreaded to see them leave for their distant courts. But he had other sons with him for consolation. Charles, the heir apparent, hailed as "the hope, the glory of the kingdom," was almost constantly at court. "Like his father in manner and appearance, he was from an early age entrusted with important military missions, creating for himself a reputation for bravery greater than a lion." Charles never married, although his father tried unsuccessfully on one occasion to arrange a union for him with the daughter of King Offa of Mercia. Also present at Aix were the infants Drogo, Hugo, and Theodoric, all of whom Charlemagne "loved well."

With his daughters Charlemagne did not sacrifice his fatherly urge to be surrounded by his offspring. According to Einhard, "they were so beautiful and were loved so much by him that, strange to say, he was not willing to give any of them in marriage either within or outside the kingdom, but kept all of them with him in his home until his death, saying that he could not live without them." The King did consent to the bethrothal of the infant Rotrud to the Byzantine Emperor Constantine VI in 781 and allowed a Greek to come to the Frankish court to instruct the princess. But the marriage never took place because of mounting political hostilities. Thereafter, he would not tolerate the suggestion of marriage. For example, in 790 he sent a legate to England to negotiate a marriage between his son and the daughter of King Offa. The Mercian king "would not agree unless Berta, daughter of Charles the Great, be given to his son in marriage, at which the most powerful king was so angry that he ordered that nobody from the British island or the nation of the English should land on the coast of Gaul for the purpose of trade."

Instead of permitting his daughters normal marriages,

Charlemagne kept them as adornments of his court. Whether his efforts to educate them in the arts, practical pursuits, and virtue were successful is not clear. What his daughters did possess were beauty, charm, and social grace which made them attractive fixtures in the predominantly male atmosphere of the court. Their physical beauty was a constant theme of the court poets. Their extravagant tastes in clothing added brightness to court life. They could ride in the hunt, join painlessly in the exuberant atmosphere prevailing at the royal table, and act with decorum when solemn occasion demanded. These were the qualities which prompted Alcuin to write that "fortunate indeed is the father who produces from his seed such flowers." In saying this, Alcuin had to overlook the fact that two of Charlemagne's daughters bore illegitimate children: Rotrud a son by a prominent count, and Berta two sons by Angilbert, court favorite, royal confidant, poet, and eventually abbot of an important monastery. The conduct of the other daughters was probably no better, for when Louis the Pious succeeded Charlemagne, one of his first acts was to compel his sisters and half-sisters to leave the court for a convent. Yet while Charlemagne reigned, none of this bothered the court circle. It is difficult to understand Charlemagne's tolerance of misconduct by his daughters and his refusal to permit them normal marriages unless one concludes that they so enlivened his court and so amused him and his confidants that he would overlook anything rather than part with them.

The family circle was further enlarged by other relatives. One of whom Charlemagne was especially fond was his sister Gisela, abbess of Chelles, but often at court, where she joined the feast and "got a sweet kiss from her brother." At various times Charlemagne's cousins frequented the court for long periods—Adalard, Wala, and Gundrada, the last called "a familiar of the King, most noble among nobles, who remained pure among all the passion of the palace." When Pepin, king of Italy, died in 810, leaving a son and five daughters, "the King showed the full extent of his piety when he allowed the son to succeed to the kingdom of his father, and caused his granddaughters to be educated among his own daughters." These young girls found other grandchildren at court, as we learn from a touching poem sent to court by Abbot Angilbert to inquire whether his bastard sons by Berta were growing and expressing a fatherly urge to see them playing in the palace garden.

Almost as strong as the bond of blood was the tie of friendship which drew to Aix a circle of men attractive to the King and made them full participants in the intimate affairs of the royal household. Einhard noted that Charlemagne "showed a fine disposition in his friendships, embracing them readily, maintaining them faithfully, and treating with the greatest respect all whom he admitted into his circle of friends." One rule seems to have governed the composition of this group: it was constituted of those whom the King found attractive to himself. Certainly profession made no difference, for royal intimates included scholars, artists, warriors, administrators, abbots, and bishops. Neither did nationality, since Englishmen, Spaniards, Italians, and Irishmen mingled freely with Franks. No single mentality—for example, the clerical or the martial—ever dominated. What we know of some of the chief court figures suggests that Charlemagne loved variety in his friends.

Alcuin, for example, was serious, a little pedantic, moralistic, and never very imaginative, while Angilbert was brilliant, worldly, perceptive, capable of decision and action, facile, and perhaps amoral. Theodulf, a Goth from Spain, was sophisticated, widely read, sharp in his ability to see the failings of others, witty, and genuinely humanistic, while Einhard, called the "dwarf" in the court circle, was a practical doer of small things, a keen observer of details, never brilliant but always busy. Taken together, the royal friends represented a fair cross section of the elite in Frankish society brought together by their personal attachment to Charlemagne. He dominated them completely; all who shared his table and his hall accepted his lordship. There is little evidence of strong factionalism within the court circle. Nor is there proof that a dominant feature of court life was sycophancy. Charlemagne was constantly being praised, but seldom did flattery decide his course of action. Theodulf, for example, might describe his master's mind as "wider than the Nile, greater than the icy Ister, larger than the Euphrates, and not less than the Ganges," but it was the quick-witted Spaniard's unique talents, his loyalty, and his service rather than his agile tongue that made him a royal "friend" and a powerful court figure.

The atmosphere prevailing at court was intimate, informal, and spontaneous. Charlemagne was not inclined toward ceremony and protocol except where political, religious, or diplomatic situations demanded a degree of pomp. He was a man of action, and it was incessant activity that characterized court life. "The iron Charles" was himself possessed of tremendous energy which permitted him over the course of his long reign to pursue an incredible round of activity that would have destroyed a lesser man. Einhard provides this description of the King: "His body was large and robust. In stature he was tall, but not ungainly—for his height was seven times the length of his own feet [about six feet, three inches]. The top of his head was round, and he had large and piercing eyes. His nose was somewhat larger than average. His hair was light and beautiful and his face was friendly and joyful. Thus whether sitting or standing he possessed authority and dignity of appearance. Although his neck was thick and short and he had a protruding stomach, these were not evident because of the good proportions of the rest of his body. His step was firm and the whole bearing of his body was manly. His voice was clear, but not as strong as the form of his body seemed to suggest. His health was excellent, except that during the last four years of his life he had frequent fevers and toward the end he was lame in one foot." This powerful body assured that every day at court was a full one. The King's religious practices got him up early, and he was soon busy. "While he was putting on his boots and clothing," he began to consult with his friends and officials and to issue orders "just as if he were sitting in his tribunal." Far into the night the activity continued. The King was a light sleeper, waking four or five times at night and getting up each time. Sometimes there was a slight respite, for Charlemagne was accustomed during the summer to nap "for two or three hours, removing his clothing and shoes just as he did at night."

To a considerable extent the King enjoyed the pursuits

customary among his Germanic ancestors, giving court life a strong Germanic flavor. This proud attachment to the manners of his ancestors was evident in his preference in dress. Einhard wrote that "he wore the national dress of the Franks" and that on all except festive occasions "his costume was little different from that of the common people." This garb included linen undergarments, red leg wrappings, a fringed tunic, and laced boots. In the winter an otter or ermine jacket was added. A cloak, made in the form of a double square so that when it was placed over the shoulders it reached the feet in front and back and knees on the sides, was worn over the other garments; around it was bound a sword belt. On festive occasions the King wore a golden vestment, jeweled shoes, a gold girdle binding his cloak, and a jeweled golden crown. Einhard avows that the King "disliked foreign garments, no matter how beautiful, and never consented to wear them, except in Rome, where, once at the request of Pope Hadrian and another time at the supplication of Leo, his successor, he donned a long tunic, a mantle, and shoes fashioned after the custom of the Romans." Notker notes that Charlemagne was not pleased with those Franks who were abandoning their native costumes in favor of "Gallic" habit. The King tolerated this until Frisian merchants began charging the same price for the tiny Gallic cloaks as for the ample Frankish ones. Then he forbade everyone to buy the Gallic cloaks, saying: "What is the use of these little things? In bed I cannot cover myself with them, when I am on horseback I cannot protect myself from the wind and the rain, and when answering the call of nature I suffer from frozen legs."

Another reflection of the Germanic flavor of Charlemagne's court was the King's enjoyment of the banquet table. Einhard says this of royal eating habits: "With food and drink he was temperate, but especially in drinking, for he greatly disliked drunkenness in any man, and especially in himself or in his intimates. He could not abstain from food so easily, so that he often complained that fasting was injurious to the body. He rarely gave great banquets, except on the most important festivals, but then he invited a great number of people. His daily meal was served in four courses, not counting the roasts which the hunters were accustomed to bring in on spits and which he ate with more pleasure than any other food. . . . He was so temperate in the use of wine and drink of any kind that he rarely drank more than three times during a meal." The King's love for roasts was so great that even in his last years he refused to follow his doctors' advice to give them up in favor of boiled meats. Other sources verify his distaste for fasting. Notker says that a bishop once reprimanded the King for breaking his Lenten fast too early in the day. Whereupon the King —with a logic befitting a gourmet—went to great trouble to show the bishop that he ate early only so that others would not suffer, since it would take far into the night to feed everybody in the royal household in his proper turn if the King did not eat early.

From the writings of Alcuin, Theodulf, Angilbert, and Einhard, all of whom frequently sat at the royal table, emerges a delightful picture of the festive spirit surrounding the royal meals. Those who were to dine with the King gathered in the great hall of the royal residence under the supervision of the chamberlain, who bustled about receiv-

ing the guests, seating some and asking others to wait outside. The assemblage was a varied one: Franks, Goths,
Irish, and English, old and young, masters and students,
warriors and poets, clergymen and court functionaries. As
each viewed the King, the Queen, and the royal children,
he must have felt that sentiment expressed by Theodulf:
"Fortunate is he who is always able to be with [the King]."
While awaiting the command to dine, the royal sons and
daughters ministered to their father in small ways: took his
sword and cloak, offered him flowers, smiled at him, or
offered a pleasantry. Visitors received warm greetings and
exchanged gifts with their friends. Theodulf regaled a circle
of guests with remarks about the talent of some who
claimed to be poets; he reminded Angilbert that "a parrot
ruins his muse with imitations of poetry" and asked, "What
can the swans do while the crows make such noises?" The
diminutive Einhard and his fellow students darted in and
out, bringing books to their elders and jotting notes for
important figures. Charlemagne certainly joined this conversation, for he "was fluent and ready in speech . . . so
fluent that he seemed loquacious."

The meal began on royal signal. After a blessing by the
royal chaplain, the food was brought under the supervision of the sweating chief steward, who, "coming in often
surrounded by troops of bakers and cooks, held forth as if
conducting a court of law; doing everything prudently, he
displayed the many dishes before the honored seat of the
king." Some guests required special dishes; Alcuin, for instance, had porridge and cheese. The royal treasurer poured
wine for all, while the slow-footed "Lentulus" passed fruit
amidst jovial reminders to hurry. "And in the middle David

ruled over all, dispensing large servings with calm order."

Conversation flowed freely during the meal. Perhaps Alcuin was its chief prompter, for he was eternally the schoolmaster. He probably tried to keep the discussion serious, but with small success. Theodulf demanded that he put aside his porridge and take wine so that he could teach and sing better, a sally that must have caused merriment, since Alcuin was an admitted lover of wine. Occasionally the conversation was interrupted for reading a poem. This caused the hulking Wido, probably a count, to put his hands to his head and to scowl at the reader until the King's glance reminded him of his manners. Even worse for this boorish noble and his ilk must have been the readings from Augustine's *City of God*, which the King enjoyed during his meals. Perhaps the worst fate for Wido was to be called upon to read aloud, for Notker says that Charlemagne insisted that everyone be prepared to take his turn at reading. However, if the Widos could suffer through the brilliant repartee, the poetic recitations, and the reading of philosophy—seeking solace in food and drink—they might ultimately be entertained to suit their tastes. Histories, poems, and songs celebrating the deeds of ancient warriors were recited during meals. Alcuin notes in disapproving tones that mimes, dancers, tellers of tales, and musicians were always present at court and were enjoyed—too much, he thought—by such important figures as Angilbert. And so the feast extended far into the night. Nothing suggests that the King restrained this happy fellowship; in fact, he enjoyed it as much as or more than the others.

Feasting often provided the aftermath of a vigorous hunting expedition, for the chase was one of Charlemagne's greatest pleasures. Einhard wrote that "he exercised himself assiduously in riding and hunting, which was a national habit with the Franks and there was hardly another people on earth that could equal them in this." Few autumns, including the one just before Charlemagne's death in January, 814, passed without a royal hunting trip lasting a month or two. Whenever the King was at Aix, he hunted frequently in the park near the palace. These forays were lively affairs. They began early in the morning, when the courtyard of the palace was filled with neighing horses and fierce dogs straining at the leashes with which peasants held them. After the King came from mass and the Queen and the royal daughters had finally finished their elaborate dressing ritual, the party set off amidst the sound of horns and the baying of the hounds. Ultimately a bear or stag was raised, and the chase began with the King on his spirited steed in the van. And he was present at the kill, often dispatching the cornered animal himself. The prize was but a symbol of a day well spent amidst friends who enjoyed the exhilarating activity of the hunt—the horses, the dogs, the noise, the costumes, the chase, and the gory, action-filled kill.

Whenever he was at Aix, the King also spent many hours swimming, "at which he was so skilled that no one could justly be called his superior." His love for companionship again manifested itself, for Einhard says he invited his sons, his nobles, his friends, his followers, and his bodyguards to join him in the bath house, "so that often a hundred or more men bathed at one time." Swimming was mixed with conversation, probably light, frivolous, and jovial at most times, but serious on some occasions. Alcuin, for example, wrote that on one occasion he discussed with the King the allegorical meaning of certain numbers recorded in Scripture while the two were in the bath.

Interspersed among the vigorous amusements of court life was an incessant round of religious activity for which Charlemagne set the model. His personal piety evoked constant praise from his admirers, most of whom would have enthusiastically praised the bishops who at a synod in 813 thanked the Lord for giving them "a chief who surpassed all the other kings of the earth by his holy wisdom and his pious zeal." This "pious zeal" found expression in many ways. The King was "most devout in sustaining the impoverished and in free giving, which the Greeks call alms giving." Those who benefited ranged from "the poor on the squares and street corners" of Aix to the Christians of Syria, Egypt, and Africa. Among Charlemagne's most impressive acts of piety was the construction of the new church at Aix, an act supplemented by his generosity in contributing to the building and adornment of a number of other churches in his realm. Einhard wrote that "as long as his health permitted, he frequented the church [at Aix] with great diligence, attending morning and evening services, the nocturnal hours, and the sacrifice of the mass." Notker pictures him leaving his bed chamber in a long, flowing robe to meet the clergy waiting outside the church for the nocturnal services. Even the hunt was preceded by attendance at mass. The King took a personal interest in the propriety of the clerical vestments and correctness of the liturgy used in his church. Probably he felt righteous and a little proud at the solemn splendor with which such feasts as Christmas and Easter were celebrated. On such occasions a magnificent procession formed in the royal residence. Soldiers led the procession across the palace court, clearing a path through the crowds. The master of the guards personally escorted the King, the Queen, the royal children, the great court officials, and the noble guests. Near the church the assembled clergy, resplendently garbed, awaited the royal party and led it into the church. As the solemn service unfolded in the majestic setting of the new church, the King joined his voice in the singing, prayed with the others, and undoubtedly felt near to God. Probably so solemn were such events that even unexpected occurrences, such as the collapse of the passageway joining the church and the royal residence while Louis the Pious was returning from Easter services, could not break the pious spell.

If one seeks to penetrate this formidable outward display of religiosity in search of the inner quality of Charlemagne's religious life, he is confronted by puzzling contradictions. In many ways the "most Christian king" appeared as a dedicated reformer aspiring to a more profound grasp of Christianity; his efforts in this direction were so notable that separate consideration must be given to them. Yet simultaneously he participated fully in an order of religious practice that seems primitive and almost childish. He was an avid collector of relics and a confirmed believer in their efficacy. When he heard in 804 that the blood of Christ had been found in Mantua, he hurriedly sent a message to the Pope asking him to inquire into the truth of this report. He often attested his conviction of God's direct intervention in military and political affairs. He believed that dreams and the movements of the stars held the key to future events. He missed no opportunity to visit the shrines of the saints so that he might share the benefits accruing to those who frequented these holy places. He was anxious that everybody pray for him. No doubt he was pleased to hear that Abbott Angilbert of St. Riquier (the aforementioned father of Berta's illegitimate sons) had organized a three-shift operation requiring thirty altars, three hundred monks, and one hundred clerks to provide "continuous prayer for the salvation of glorious Augustus Charles and for the long duration of his reign." He probably shared with Einhard the belief that a series of unusual events between 810 and 814 all presaged his own death.

These glimpses into the mentality behind Charlemagne's acts of "pious zeal" leave little doubt that the people of Aix, including the King, believed devoutly in the close proximity of a personal God who might reward or punish them at any moment. Their God revealed His intentions in a bewildering array of portents and signs that had best be heeded. Theological speculation and moral questions had a place in the divine scheme of things; however, they did not touch the essence of the religious spirit prevailing at Aix and all across the vast empire. Men lived in an emotion-charged world where every event was a manifestation of God, His angels, and the evil spirits, where the Day of Judgment was close at hand, where the miraculous was ordinary, where the eternal and the temporal, the supernatural and the natural merged into one. It was this sense of the proximity of the divine which pervaded every event in Aix and which provides the prime key to the Carolingian outlook. And there was no better child of the age than Charlemagne.

What has been described so far as characteristic features of Aix's social life would not have made the city especially unique; the dining hall, the hunt, the bath, the chapel were the ordinary pursuits of the Germanic nobility which dominated the Frankish state and would have prevailed at many aristocratic villas. Perhaps the royal circle at Aix followed these pursuits with greater zest, color, and aplomb than did less illustrious "courts," but it took more than these to provide Aix its distinction. Such distinction emerged from other activities which added a non-Germanic flavor to the city's life, which drew its populace into a larger world.

Especially notable on this score were the intellectual pursuits that played a significant part in the daily life of the court. Charlemagne had a passion for learning that set him apart from his predecessors and manifested itself in ways that had a profound influence on his personal conduct. Einhard indicated the general tenor of his intellectual interests: "He was fluent and ready in speech and could express with great clearness whatever he wished. Not content with only his native language, he also undertook the task of learning foreign languages. Among these he mastered Latin so that he was accustomed to speak equally in that and his own tongue; however, he was able to understand Greek better than speak it. . . . He studied the liberal arts most assiduously, and admiring greatly the teachers of the arts, he bestowed on them great honors. In the learning of grammar he listened to Peter, the aged deacon of Pisa. In the other disciplines he had as a teacher Albinus, called Alcuin, likewise a deacon, a most learned man of Saxon descent from Britain. He spent much time and labor

82

with Alcuin in learning rhetoric, dialectic, and especially astronomy. He also studied the art of computing and investigated with eager intention and great curiosity the course of the stars. And he tried to learn to write; for this purpose he was accustomed to keep tablets and little books in his bed under his pillow, so that, when he had free time, he could train his hand by tracing the letters. However, his efforts, begun too late and disorganized, had little success."

The King's urge to learn brought to court a group of teachers who represented the best talent in several branches of learning. This group of scholars and teachers, swelled by those officials, clergymen, and royal friends interested in learning, constituted what has sometimes been called the "palace academy," although that designation implies a greater degree of formal organization than the group possessed. Its composition changed constantly as one or another scholar or teacher left to become a bishop or abbot, as young men were added, as court officials departed for a mission in some remote part of the kingdom. Meetings were irregular and extremely informal, often occurring during the course of feasts, in the bath, or in the royal bed chamber. There was no formal program or any set subject to occupy the gathering. An air of preciousness, of vanity, of pretentiousness may have possessed the group, as is suggested by the special names assigned to each member: Charlemagne was David, Alcuin was Flaccus, Angilbert was Homer, Einhard was Bezaleel. Alcuin justified this gesture by saying that "close friendships often call for a change of names," and by citing the example of Christ and His disciples.

The irregularity, the informality, and the self-consciousness surrounding the activities of the court "intellectuals" must not detract from their genuine interest in learning or from their impact on their age. The members of the academy eagerly listened to and praised or criticized the latest poetic creation of one of the circle. All participated in serious debates on theological questions, pooling their knowledge to correct one another's views. The presentation of a new idea gleaned from a book just acquired at the court was a special occasion. These encounters undoubtedly broadened the perspectives of all and sharpened their concepts. None was a more avid participant than Charlemagne. Often he played the role of questioner, seeking to extract from his learned friends all kinds of information. He had a special passion for learning more about astronomy and for fathoming the hidden meanings of Scripture. Sometimes he was not satisfied with the answers of his friends at court and wrote to others for more information. One can almost imagine his glee when he could confront his "academicians" with the results of his private inquiries. Charlemagne certainly did not confine himself entirely to the learner's role. He acted as an equal in intelligence, taste, and knowledge to the rest of the academy. That he was capable of matching wits with his learned friends or was fully appreciative of their aesthetic tastes is not clear, since nobody was eager to record anything that would detract from his position as king and patron. What is amazing is that a man burdened with immense responsibilities of state and inclined by temperament to a vigorous, active life would so enjoy the serious intellectual and artistic pursuits of the "palace academy." Many of his companions of the battlefield, the hunt, and the banquet table must have counted lost the hours spent talking of poetry, theology, grammar, logic, history, and astronomy. They could hardly have denied, however, that this search for refinement and sophistication constituted a significant part of the total atmosphere prevailing at Aix.

A constant stream of foreign visitors also helped to extend the vision of Aix's citizens. Einhard said that the King "had a great love for foreigners and went to such great pains to entertain them that in all justice their numbers seemed to be a burden not only to the palace but to the whole kingdom." A sampling from the chroniclers of the age will supply an indication of the frequency of the appearance of foreigners at Aix. In 796 the newly elected pope, Leo III, sent to the King by his legates "the keys to the confession of St. Peter and the flag of the city along with other gifts." In the same year an Avar prince and a great following, "with their long hair flowing behind them," came to receive baptism and to submit to the Franks. In the early summer of 797 the Moslem prince of Barcelona appeared at Aix to make his submission and to give over his city. Later in the same year the son of the Unmayad ruler of Spain arrived to seek Frankish help. Also from Spain in 798 came the legates of Alfonso, the Christian ruler of Galicia and Asturia, bringing "cloaks, mules, and Moorish prisoners as insignia" of a recent victory won by Alfonso. In 798 and 799 envoys from the Byzantine Empire visited Aix and were given dignified and friendly receptions. In 799 "a certain monk came from Jerusalem and brought blessings and relics from the sepulcher of the Lord which the Patriarch of Jerusalem sent to the Lord King." Perhaps no legation caused so much stir as did the one which came in 802. The *Royal Annals* record that "in this year on July 20 there came Isaac with an elephant and other gifts which were sent by the king of the Persians [the Abbasid Caliph Harun-al-Rashid]." The elephant, named Abul Abaz, provided "a wonderful spectacle"; its death a few years later warranted recording in several annals. Harun-al-Rashid also sent "monkeys, balsam, nard, unguents of various kinds, spices, scents, and many drugs, all in such profusion that it seemed as if the East had been left bare so that the West might be filled."

The reception of these foreigners called for special measures. From the pen of Notker comes an imaginative reconstruction of the events connected with the visit of an embassy of Harun-al-Rashid at Aix. The Persians arrived at Aix "weary and footsore," having spent "a whole year after their landing in Italy trying to reach the Frankish court, their journey being complicated by the deceit and the rudeness of the bishops and abbots of Italy and Gaul."

"They arrived in the last week of Lent. Their arrival having been made known to the Emperor, he postponed their presentation until Easter evening. Then when that incomparable monarch was dressed with the greatest magnificence for the most important of all feasts, he ordered that the envoys of that race which once was so terrible to the whole world be introduced. But the sight of the most magnificent Charles so terrified them that one would think they had never seen a king or emperor before. Having received them in a most kindly way, he granted them this privilege—that they might go wherever they wanted to, just as if they were his own sons, and might look at anything and ask whatever questions or make any inquiries they

chose. They leaped with joy at this favor, and they valued
the privilege of clinging close to Charles, of gazing upon
him, admiring him above all the wealth of the East. They
went up into the ambulatory that runs around the nave
of the cathedral and looked down on the clergy and soldiers. Then they returned to the Emperor, and because of
their great joy, they could not refrain from laughing aloud.
Clapping their hands, they said: 'We have seen only men
of clay before; here are men of gold.' Then going to the
nobles one by one, they admired with wonder the novelty
of their arms and garments. They passed that night and the
next Sunday in church. On the holy day itself they were
invited by the most munificent Charles to a splendid banquet, along with all the nobles of Francia and Europe.
There they were so struck by the wonder of everything that
they had hardly eaten anything at the end of the banquet."

As further entertainment Charlemagne organized a hunt,
during the course of which he and some of his nobles displayed a bravery that astounded the envoys. The visitors'
courage left something to be desired, for "when they saw
the immense animals, they were so stricken with fear that
they fled." And the King engaged them in conversations.
During one of these discussions the legates, "in a particularly merry mood and a little heated by too much beer,"
even suggested that the real power of Charlemagne was
not so great as it was reputed to be in the East, as was
evidenced by the way his nobles and clergy treated foreigners when he was not present. Perhaps this brashness
was not especially welcome after such strenuous efforts to
impress upon the foreigners the magnificence of the Franks.

During the rare intervals when no important foreign

legation was present or expected at Aix, the court could find a substitute by listening to the tales of Frankish legates who had returned from a foreign expedition. Such journeys were numerous, and the experience was long and arduous. Emissaries sent to Constantinople were often gone for a year, while those dispatched to Baghdad did not return for nearly four years. Such extended stays provided the travelers with amazing stories to recount at Aix. Some indication of these accounts is contained in a poem written by Bishop Amalarius of Trier on his return from Constantinople in 814. It speaks of a cruel sea journey, a none-too-kindly treatment in Constantinople, an interview with the Byzantine emperor, an even worse journey home, and the joys of seeing Italy again. An artful voyager could easily expand any of these adventures into a tale which might entrance the court circle for an entire evening.

Aix was sometimes the scene of an order of events which bred a heightened spirit of jubilation arising out of a sense that the destiny of the Franks was at stake. The reports of military victories occasioned this reaction. That the outcome of each campaign was anxiously awaited by those left behind is attested by Alcuin, who declined to take part in military expeditions because, as he put it, "what would a hare do among the bears, a lamb among the lions?" but who constantly inquired by letter for news about royal expeditions. Sometimes news of victory reached those left behind by letter from the battlefield, as was the case in 791 when Charlemagne announced his victory over the Avars in a letter to Queen Fastrada. This was no substitute for the appearance of the victors; for example, Charlemagne's arrival at Aix in 798 with 1,600 Saxon nobles seized as hostages during a summer campaign or the arrival in 795 of fifteen wagons so heavily loaded with Avar gold and silver that four oxen were needed to pull each one. In a lengthy passage in his *Poem in Honor of Louis the Pious*, Ermoldus Nigellus recreates the sentiment prevailing at Aix when news of the taking of Barcelona in 801 reached Aix. A participant named Bigo hurried to court, where the joyful news was quickly spread. Charlemagne called the messenger to his presence and quizzed him about every detail of the victory. Having given thanks to God, the Emperor then asked again for all the particulars about the campaign. The vicarious thrill of reliving the battle and the relief felt by all impregnate this account. One senses that the elation which moved "the joyful emperor" was felt throughout the city and was not dissipated for days.

Another event symbolizing the destiny of the Franks occurred in Aix in 813. This was the designation of Louis as Charlemagne's successor and his formal elevation to the emperorship. Several accounts describing this event indicate that the suspense began to build when Charlemagne, "weakened by sickness and old age," summoned Louis to Aix and instructed him in his new responsibilities. Then, in September, Charlemagne summoned his magnates and announced that, because "[his] blood had slowed, the hard burdens of age had slowed [him], white hair framed [his] pale visage, [his] warlike right arm, once famous throughout the world, now fell trembling as icy blood coursed through it," it was time to designate a successor. "All who were at Aix rejoiced: the clergy, the people, the nobles, the father." Then came the actual coronation on the following Sunday in the church at Aix. Regally outfitted, the aging father rose to address his son on his duties, and Louis responded that he would follow his father's advice. Whereupon Charlemagne took from the altar a gold crown and placed it on his son's head. Then the two heard mass and returned to the palace, the son supporting his father. A great feast followed. The rapturous words of Ermoldus Nigellus probably reflect the sentiments of the city populace as they celebrated the perpetuation of the dynasty of Charlemagne: "Oh! a festive day remembered for years. Land of Francia, these are the emperors you possess. Applaud, Francia! and likewise let golden Rome applaud, for all the other nations admire that empire."

Although the streets and squares of Aix most often reflected the happy mood of the hunt, the feast, the military or diplomatic triumph, the pageantry of high politics, there were moments when other sentiments prevailed. Real terror must have seized the city in the winter of 802–803 when "an earthquake shook the palace and the surrounding territory and many deaths resulted." At times a spirit of vague foreboding, engendered by signs of disorder in nature, gripped the city. Plagues, droughts, extreme cold, crop failures, floods, and hailstorms all were signs to cause alarm. Wild rumors sometimes spread to agitate the populace. For example, a plague which in 810 wiped out large numbers of cattle led to the rumor that a royal enemy had caused the disaster by sending his agents through the kingdom to scatter a lethal dust "in the mountains and fields, the pastures and wells." Agitated emotions bred violence; a royal order of 810 commanded the King's agents "to inquire concerning the murders committed in the present year by ignorant men, murders prompted by the deadly dust." These incidents suggest a highly emotional populace in Aix; men buoyed up by success and pageantry could be cast into despair by some natural occurrence or accident interpreted as a sign of divine wrath.

Aix also knew days of deep mourning. The death of Pope Hadrian I on Christmas, 795, caused Charlemagne "to weep as if he had lost a beloved brother or son." The deaths of two trusted military commanders, Gerold, count of Pannonia, and Erich, duke of Friuli, in 799 and of Queen Liutgard in 800 apparently moved the King and his courtiers deeply if we can judge from the epitaphs written to commemorate these losses. What Charlemagne felt most deeply, however, was the passing of his children. Between June 4, 810, and December 4, 811, four of them died unexpectedly, all in the full bloom of life: Pepin the Hunchback, Rotrud, the second Pepin, and Charles. Einhard wrote that the King "suffered these deaths less patiently than might be expected for one of such magnanimity of character; his love for them compelled him to tears." All in Aix probably wept at the cruel fate suffered by the aging king.

The deepest mourning of the city, however, came early in 814. After his customary hunting trip in the fall of 813, the lame and weakened king returned to Aix in November. In January he was stricken with a fever after bathing. The court doctors probably reacted in a fashion suggested by Alcuin in one of his poems: "The doctors, the Hippocratic sect, rush about. One opens a vein, while another mixes herbs in a pot. A third cooks a broth, while still another brings forth a potion." Although Charlemagne was accustomed "to follow his own will rather than the advice of doctors," he did undertake a fast. But the fever mounted and his body grew weaker from lack of food. Then he was seized by pleurisy. On the seventh day he summoned his friend, the Archchaplain Hilduin, for the last rites. After receiving communion, "he struggled in his illness that day and the following night. The next morning, as light came, still knowing what he was doing, he raised his right arm with what strength he could muster and made the sign of the cross on his head, his breast, and his whole body. Then he drew his feet together, folded his arms and hands over his body, closed his eyes, and sang softly, 'Into your hands, O Lord, I commend my soul.' Immediately after he died in peace." The annals record that on that day, January 28, there was great weeping among all people. Charlemagne's body was washed and oiled and carried to the church amidst the lamentations of the people; there it was buried on the same day.

Well might the people of Aix weep, for their city would never be the same again. During the twenty years preceding his death Charlemagne had been the animating force in the "second Rome." No more would his presence highlight the activities of the banquet hall, the hunt, the bathing party, the religious ceremonies, the military triumph, and the reception of foreign diplomats. No longer would his imposing physical presence and strong will provide a bulwark against real or expected disasters. What the city would perhaps miss most was his constant personal participation in the small happenings around his court. To know that Charlemagne made a practice of looking down from a window in his private chamber on the activities of the palace courtyard must have constrained many in their activities;

perhaps some even suffered the chagrin of being reprimanded for certain indiscretions committed when they
thought the King would not see them. Many noble youths
attending the palace school may have remembered all their
lives the outcome of a personal examination of their literary
skills conducted by the Emperor. When their performance
proved inferior to that of the lads of middle and low birth,
the Emperor delivered an angry rebuke to the future leaders
of the kingdom. Perhaps all laughed for years at the im-
petuous young man, who, upon receiving an episcopal
apointment, was so eager to show his vigor that he rushed
out of the palace and leaped on his horse so violently that
he nearly fell off the other side. And who would forget the
time Charlemagne conspired with a Jewish merchant to
sell an avaricious bishop a mouse stuffed with spice at an
exorbitant price?

These anecdotes, products of the legend-making that
began to develop around Charlemagne even before his
death, reinforce what our previous glimpses of life in Aix
point to as the fundamental characteristics of Carolingian
society. It was a society whose chief cohesive bond was the
influence of strong individuals over a circle of dependents.
In this personal bond was an antidote for the restlessness
that had plagued Western European society since its Ro-
manized population had been deprived of its moorings
by the collapse of the Roman imperial government and
since the Germanic invaders had suffered the dissolution
of ancient tribal bonds during the era of their migrations.
Life in Aix reveals a robust energy; this was no effete society,
caught up in a round of sacred habits and empty rituals.
Gone is the ennui of the late Roman era and the undisci-

plined bursts of action punctuated with hopeless lethargy characteristic of the post-invasion Germanic courts. The energy bursting forth in Aix gained zest from an accompanying willingness to try new things. The fascination with novel art styles, literature, and peoples served to breed a state of mind willing to explore, experiment, seek the unique. The pioneers at Aix barely opened Pandora's box, but what Oswald Spengler called the "Faustian mind" may well have had its European origins in those tentative stirrings felt in the society of Aix. Finally, Aix's social activity reflected a society that was nourished by hope. Charlemagne and his circle believed that God was on their side. This faith generated a primitive "idea of progress," a concept without which Western European history is incomprehensible. Perhaps this explains why St. Augustine was a favorite of Charlemagne, for the great African bishop had distilled in his *City of God* a vision of God's promise of a golden age *in the future*. In the troubled years between the fifth century, when he wrote his book, and the age of Charlemagne, his promise seemed sterile. With the men who built and lived in Aix the hope was reborn.

# fOUR

## "CHIEF SEAT OF THE KINGDOM"

THE SOCIAL PAGEANT of Aix provides insight into some aspects of life in the age of Charlemagne, but it hardly reveals the major interest of society's leading figures. They were men inspired by a sense of mission which made them hard workers. In no pursuit were they more deadly serious than in politics; their political efforts supply a prime clue to Aix's role as a center of civilization.

A modern investigator is tempted to approach political life in Aix from a modern perspective. He is inclined to see the political issues and evaluate the political activity of the age of Charlemagne in terms of an overexpanded state, of ill-defined and poorly guarded frontiers, of a crude administrative machine, of cultural and ethnic fissures dividing the population, of economic fragmentation, and of a barbaric lack of respect for law. But the Carolingian political masters, blessed neither with the advantage of hindsight nor with the modern "science" of politics, would hardly have thought of the political issues of their age in these terms. One must turn to their own political ideology for insight into their concept of the issues of the age and of the ends proper to political action.

Carolingian political ideology was shaped with a realistic appraisal of the failures of the earlier rulers of the West well in mind. In spite of a deep pride in the glorious history of the Frankish race, the Carolingians were aware of the tragic failure of the Merovingians. So keen was this sense of past failure that most politically sensitive men felt that they lived amidst "wild tempests" which endangered the very existence of society. They sensed and expressed fear: fear that hostile foreigners would inundate the Frankish world, fear that evil men would pervert justice, fear that heretics would corrupt the weak, fear that sin would extinguish virtue, fear that an angry God would render justice upon a deficient society. This psychology is nowhere more obvious than in the letters of Alcuin, who never ceased to express a gnawing sense of insecurity. Even in the triumphal year of 800 he wrote: "These are dangerous times, and tribulation follows upon tribulation. The people are afflicted with hardship, the princes are in labor, the Church has great burdens, the priests quarrel; everything is in turmoil." Yet hope mingled with fear and fed on Charlemagne's successes. Somewhat timidly men began to consider what the good society should be like. They looked to the past for a prototype and discovered it in the political ideals of the patristic age. As a consequence, their political concepts are thoroughly theologized and theocratized. The Old Testament and *The City of God* became handbooks supplying political guidance; David and Constantine emerged as the heroes to be emulated.

The theologizing of political concepts laid down certain foundations upon which Carolingian political life was reared. Basic to the new ideology was the assumption that there existed an orderly cosmos over which God ruled absolutely. During a golden age in the past, terrestial society had operated in harmony with the perfect cosmic order.

Through his original sin man had challenged God's authority and upset the cosmic harmony; his persistence in sinning deepened the earthly disorder and widened the breach between heaven and earth. Through revelation God had provided the laws for restoring harmony. More important, God had sent His Son to lead in the restitution of earthly compliance with divine authority. The Carolingians conceived of Christ more as a powerful leader in the war against evil than as a suffering victim sacrificed for man's sins; He was Christ the King leading His troops in a war against the forces of disorder, the commanding Christ installed in the dome at Aix.

From this view of the cosmic economy Carolingian thinkers deduced that the coming of Christ had instituted a new community made up of all who through baptism accepted Christ, a new commonwealth destined to complete the task of reharmonizing terrestial with celestial society. The rediscovery of the idea that the faithful constituted a corporate entity with a unique goal was perhaps the most fertile political concept of the Carolingian age and one that Carolingian society as a whole never comprehended. It permitted the chief political figures to transcend the older Germanic view that the state was that which the king "owned" by right of conquest and could dispose as he saw fit. By envisioning the state as an organic community beyond any man, the Carolingians found justification for a political program that transcended the private interests of a single man.

A formidable array of authorities could be cited to illustrate the emerging consciousness among the Carolingians of the existence of a superior political entity, of a Christian commonwealth, to which they owed their allegiance. Especially provocative in nourishing this idea were the events leading up to Charlemagne's coronation in 800 and the effort to justify this event after it had happened. Lack of space forbids that this evidence be collected here, but perhaps one example will convey the fundamental sense of the Carolingian idea of the Christian commonwealth. It comes from the pen of Bishop Agobard of Lyons, a dedicated defender of the ideal of unity during the troubled reign of Louis the Pious.

In a letter seeking to persuade Louis to institute a unified legal system, Agobard noted that through the efforts of Christ's disciples, "one faith announced by God had been preached 'to every creature,' that is, to all the nations of the world; one hope had been diffused in the hearts of all believers by the Holy Spirit; one charity had been born in all, one will; one desire; one prayer. Thus all from different nations, diverse conditions, sexes, social ranks, and conditions of service, all say to one God the Father of all, 'Our Father, who art in Heaven, hallowed be thy name.' " After expounding on the way all men "invoke one Father, seek one sanctification, demand one king, desire one fulfillment of God's will as it is done in heaven, pray to be given daily bread," Agobard paraphrased Paul to insist that under the new dispensation there " 'is no longer Gentile and Jew, circumcized and non-circumcized, barbarian and Scythian,' Aquitanian and Lombard, Burgundian and Alemannian, 'servant and freeman, but all are one in Christ'!"

With a formidable array of scriptural citations he drove home his crucial idea: the unity of the new community created by the coming of Christ. Then he struck the fundamental note: "If the Lord afterwards suffered so that by His blood He could draw together those who were far apart, and so that the wall of division would be removed, enmity would be killed in each, and all would be reconciled to God in one body . . . , I want to know from your piety whether the great diversity of laws which exists not only in various regions and cities but even in many households does not in every way stand contrary to this divine work. For it often happens that if five men walk or sit together, not one of them will have a common law with any other in their worldly affairs, although in eternal matters they are held together by one law of Christ." Agobard then urged the Emperor to correct this intolerable disparity, reminding him that "all who have one father in God are brothers and sons of God."

From these speculations on the configuration and destiny of "Christian society" emerged sharper ideas on the King's role. The Carolingians had inherited a concept of monarchy that was strongly Germanic. The King enjoyed unlimited authority because his prowess as a warrior allowed him to create a personal patrimony of land and peoples. Within the limits of his ability he could do whatever he chose with his "property"; he was the absolute lord of his territory and of a body of dependents. Under the influence of religious ideas the Carolingians began to purge monarchy of its personal, private character. They envisaged kingship as an institution created by God as a terrestial instrumentality for ordering the affairs of sinful men in conformity with divine commands. A certain Catulf put it this way in a letter to Charlemagne: "Remember always, my king, to have fear and love of God your king, because

you stand in His place to rule and care for all His members."
Bishop Jonas of Orléans spoke even more pointedly: "No
king ought to think that he holds his kingdom from his
ancestors, but he should believe humbly that he holds it in
truth from God. . . . He who in the temporal order commands others ought to believe that sovereign power has
been entrusted to him not by men but by God." For those
less articulate, a concrete historical case—that of David—
conveyed the idea of the divine institution of monarchy
and of the obligation of the king to act in accordance with
divine commands.

The Carolingian political theorists fail us when it comes
to translating the God-given authority of their rulers into
precise statements of royal duty, perhaps because their
models failed them at the point where principles must be
articulated into specific political actions. They speak eloquently on the great burdens imposed upon those chosen
to represent God as the earthly "rectors of the Christians,"
and they cry out in fear when rulers appeared to fail in the
exercise of their stewardship. They admonished the kings
to be good and wise. Yet they did not set down the specific
practical obligations of the king in the discharge of his
divinely ordained responsibilities.

Despite this absence of detailed discussions of royal duty,
one senses from the totality of Carolingian political sources
—tracts, laws, letters, narrative accounts, and poetry—that
those in crucial political positions did have a definite sense
of the ends to which royal power should be applied. A
theologian of the era of Louis, Sedulius Scottus, condensed
into a few words the fundamental concept defining the
duty of God's vice-regents: "In so much as the good ruler

recognizes that he has been appointed by God, to that extent he watches with pious anxiety that he may before God and man arrange and weigh all things in good order according to the scales of righteousness." The vital words in this statement are "good order according to the scales of righteousness." The central duty of the king was to bring order out of confusion and disorder by imposing Christian conduct on his subjects. The norms had been defined by the great moral authorities of the past—Holy Scripture, Augustine, Ambrose, Gregory the Great, and Isidore. With the help of powerful churchmen, the king must apply this "law" in his own setting. His was the burden of Christianizing every aspect of life; this was the path that led back toward the harmony that God intended for terrestial society. His was the right to claim every power needed to achieve this end; this was God's intention in instituting monarchy. His was the terrible responsibility of having to stand judgment before God for his stewardship; this was assurance that his absolutism would not be capricious and tyrannical.

While the new ideology was highly significant in supplying purpose and direction to the wielders of power, it hardly assured successful political action capable of imposing order where disorder existed. To translate their ideals into reality, the Carolingian rulers had to depend on a governmental machine which supplied the chief tangible evidence of political life at Aix. Although crude by comparison with other systems of government, this machine was for the Carolingians sanctioned by long usage, and it seemed to them adequate as an instrumentality for attaining their political ends.

The nerve center of the governmental machinery was what the Carolingians called the *palatium*, which can be defined as a group of people who served the king and thus were constantly in his presence. Every member of this group, whether nobleman or commoner, clergyman or layman, Frank or non-Frank, free or unfree, was essentially a royal servant, bound to serve until the king released him from his obligation. It was this personal attachment to the king which provided the *palatium* with its corporate existence and which reminds us of the persistence of Germanic political traditions in the age of Charlemagne.

Any attempt to classify the personnel of the *palatium* becomes a nightmare for one accustomed to modern bureaucracies with their neat ranks of officials classed according to elaborate tables of organization. Some members of the *palatium* bore titles which suggest their functions. Among those often mentioned were the officers who had the responsibility for provisioning and managing the royal household—the seneschal, the cellarer, the count of the stable, the treasurer, the master of ceremonies, the hunt masters. There were three titled officials who ranked above the others and who held charges that were much more concerned with public affairs than were the duties of the household officials. The count of the palace, called by contemporaries the chief secular official of the realm, was responsible for dispensing justice in the name of the king, a task that put him in a position to scrutinize all matters brought to court. His counterpart in ecclesiastical affairs was the archchaplain. In a narrow sense the archchaplain was in charge of religious life at court and director of the court clergy. This responsibility made him the logical figure to whom religious problems of all kinds were referred, and as a consequence he exercised in the name of the king a general supervisory power over religious life in the whole realm. The chancellor was responsible for the vital task of preparing the various documents required to conduct royal affairs. Each of the titled officials was assisted by lesser officials. The grouping of minor officials under a superior in no sense constituted "departments" or "ministries" in the modern sense, for their activities were not guided by rigid procedural rules and their functions were not clearly defined. A careful scrutiny of the records indicates that the possession of a specific office had little to do with the services a royal servant might perform. The king chose those whom he trusted to perform any function for which he believed them fitted. There were no specialists in the *palatium*; there were only servants of the king.

Carolingian sources reveal another category of men intimately engaged in the vital functions of government. These men bore no titles, but were called the royal vassals (*vassi dominici*). This designation meant that they were attached to the person of the king by a special process called commendation. The exact nature of their position and of the bond created by commendation emerges only when one looks at the institution of vassalage, which supplied a fundamental underpinning not only of the *palatium* but also of the whole Carolingian political system.

In its essential features vassalage was not a public institution. It was a private agreement or contract, voluntarily entered into by two free individuals, whereby one (the vassal) bound himself under oath to serve another (the lord) in return for protection and material benefits. It had originated as an amalgam of Germanic, Roman, and Celtic practices during the unsettled years of the sixth, seventh, and eighth centuries, when weak men sought security by attaching themselves to strong individuals. As its use spread, the form and the nature of the contractural arrangement were defined more sharply and an ever broadening range of mutual services and obligations became involved. Especially significant was the gradual development of the practice of associating a material consideration with the personal union between two individuals. When a vassal pledged to serve his lord, he was given something of value, called a benefice, which permitted him to render his services and solidified his attachment to his lord.

In the course of the long period of the growth of vassalage, the Frankish kings became involved. They acquired their own vassals, including many of the chief men of their realm, who publicly pledged to serve the king as their lord. In many cases the kings granted to their vassals attractive benefices, usually in the form of land drawn from the royal domain. In return they demanded of their vassals public services, especially military service, at private expense. Charlemagne and Louis labored to extend, solidify, regularize, and make attractive the institution of vassalage as a buttress to royal power. Central to their whole policy was their effort to impose upon those commended to them the responsibility of performing public duties as a part of their obligation to their personal lord, the king. They hoped thereby to establish a pool of competent, loyal men to bear the burden of government. They drew constantly on this pool to populate the *palatium*. Some of their vassals held specific offices, but again some of the most important figures at court were vassals who occupied no office. Certain vassals spent all their time in the service of the *palatium*; others came when summoned to perform some particular duty and then returned to their private interests. In return for loyal service every royal vassal was well rewarded materially and gained an important social status; thus the acceptance of vassalage in the service of the king was made attractive.

The *palatium* was the nerve center of the political machine; the arms were the agents representing the king on the local scene. For the most part the burden of local administration was borne by two officials, the count and the bishop. The count represented the king's authority within a fixed territorial unit called the county. Chosen by the king, each served until the king relieved him. Most of the counts were drawn from the great noble families of Frankish origin which had long been intimately associated with the Carolingian dynasty; their dispersion over much of Western Europe as royal agents created a kind of super-aristocracy dedicated to the imposition of the royal will. The scope of the count's authority was virtually unlimited within his county. His ordinary functions included the administration of justice, the enforcement of royal orders, the summoning and provisioning of military contingents, the suppression of crime, and the collection of taxes. Faithful performance of these duties brought considerable reward in the form of a portion of whatever money the count collected and of grants of land made by the king. Each count was assisted by lesser officials, called vicars and centenaries, charged mainly with the administration of justice in minor cases within fixed subdivisions of the county.

Equally important in local administration was the bishop. Although a servant of the Church, every Carolingian bishop was expected to act as a royal agent in the enactment of royal edicts pertaining to religion. This obligation made him a public official. And on many other occasions the bishops were commanded to execute royal orders in matters far removed from spiritual affairs: promulgating laws, conducting courts, representing the king as diplomatic agents, collecting money, and organizing military contingents. Like the count, the bishop administered a clearly defined territorial unit, called a diocese, and was assisted by a staff of subordinates. Almost without exception and in direct contravention of canon law, Charlemagne and Louis appointed bishops, thus populating the episcopal sees with men they believed best suited to serve royal ends. In the main the bishops derived from the same aristocratic families that supplied the counts.

The rulers and their confidants fretted constantly about the quality of local officials; they took seriously the stricture of Bishop Jonas of Orléans that "it is a sin when a king entrusts the carrying out of an office to sinful judges and ministers." From a considerable body of literature devoted to the conduct of officials it is clear that Charlemagne and Louis were keenly aware of Alcuin's remark that "the sins of their subordinates could be imputed to those who are rectors." In all this literature there is a strong religious tone, illustrating the over-all tendency of Carolingian political thought to cast politics in the framework of Christian ethics. A public charge originated from God; to abuse it was a sin that would warrant severe punishment in the hereafter. The prospect that wicked officials would eventually receive retribution may have offered consolation to the victims of a reprobate like Count Bogo, who—according to the dream of an old lady—went straight to hell after his death. There a horde of demons forced him to swallow gold, insisting that he could for all eternity slake his thirst for what he had so desperately lusted after on earth. To some extent Charlemagne and Louis succeeded in elevating the quality of local officials and in inspiring their appointees with a sense of responsibility for public welfare. But the struggle was difficult, for many officials considered a royal office as a license to prey upon the public. This attitude made extremely difficult the Carolingian quest for order.

While they were at Aix, the kings spent countless hours prodding this political machine into motion. At the risk of oversimplification, we can group their activities in terms of four broad processes which encompassed the essential features of Carolingian political life: the gathering of information, the formulation of decisions, the securing of assent for action, and the imposition of decisions on the population of the empire.

In their political actions Charlemagne and Louis were extremely pragmatic, acting in terms of specific situations. Consequently, they needed to be informed about affairs in their realm. Their quest for information took many forms. They regularly made personal circuits of their realm to see for themselves what needed attention. Letters were constantly dispatched to important individuals asking for information. Great men were summoned to Aix and questioned about affairs in their areas. In his tract on the organization of the royal government Bishop Hincmar of Rheims said that the King "expressly ordered that each noble zealously inquire before coming to the king concerning the interior and exterior affairs of the kingdom, seeking information from natives as well as foreigners, from their friends as well as their enemies." All subjects were encouraged to bring their problems to court or send written complaints. Charlemagne even made a practice of drawing his courtiers from every part of his realm so that those who came to Aix seeking redress would find an acquaintance well enough positioned to assure that the complaint would be heard. Perhaps this measure succeeded too well, for a capitulary of 810 had a provision "concerning complainants who impose a great burden on the ears of the Lord Emperor at the palace."

Apparently these ways of gathering information were not adequate, for both Charlemagne and Louis made extensive use of a special group of officials, called *missi dominici*, as investigators. Earlier kings had employed *missi*, but in an irregular fashion. Charlemagne and Louis sought to regularize and universalize their activities. They divided the empire into districts and assigned to each at least two eminent and trusted men, usually a layman and a cleric, who were charged with making a circuit of their district at least once, but more ideally, four times a year. The *missi* were given specific instructions to guide their inquiries. Typical was the instruction issued to the *missi* at Aix in 802. Its forty chapters ordered an investigation into such matters as the conduct of bishops, abbots, priests, nuns, and monks, the administration of justice, the condition of the poor, the extent to which property rights were respected, the suppression of crime, and the state of royal property. The *missi* were also armed with authority to command the services of local officials. They sought to fulfill their commission by summoning the important people in their districts to assemblies and questioning them. Beyond this they were expected to make their presence known to all people and to travel as much as possible. At a specified time, usually in April of each year, the *missi* made a report to the king. Upon the receipt of the reports of those *missi* who had been assiduous and systematic, the ruler was in a position to know a great deal about the political situation in a considerable part of his realm.

Fortified with precise and reliable knowledge of conditions in the realm, the court could decide on a course of action. The ultimate power of decision rested with the king, and Charlemagne and Louis often made decisions personally, even in minor matters. But the sheer bulk of business—a badge of success for the Carolingians—demanded that many routine problems be disposed without the king's personal attention. This responsibility was entrusted to various members of the *palatium*—especially the count of the palace and the archchaplain. These officials often consulted with the rulers in disposing matters; Einhard pictures them gathering in the presence of the king while he was dressing in the morning to present problems and receive his decisions. The energetic Charlemagne undoubtedly kept close personal touch with those officials entrusted with the power of decision, thus maintaining the personal flavor of Carolingian government.

When there were great issues to decide, the Carolingian kings preferred to have advice. For this they called on a special group referred to as "counselors" or, more pompously, "senators." In his tract on royal administration

Hincmar says this of royal counselors: "Counselors were chosen, in so far as possible, from clergymen and laymen who in the first place, each according to his quality and office, feared God. Second, they were chosen because they were so faithful that—with the exception of eternal life—they put nothing above the interest of the kingdom, neither friends, enemies, parents, gifts, flatteries, nor threats. . . . The counselors thus chosen agreed among themselves and with the king that whatever discussions they had concerning the state of the kingdom or private affairs would not be revealed without the consent of all to a servant or to any other person for the length of time during which it was necessary to remain silent, be it a day or two or more, a year, or even forever. . . . The archchaplain . . . and the chancellor were always included, and therefore were always chosen with the great care, and, having been elected, were instructed so that they could take part in the council worthily. If there was found one from the other officials who showed himself fit first in listening and then in giving counsel . . . he was commanded to assist in all deliberations, paying the greatest attention to what happened, keeping secrets, learning what he did not know, and holding to that which was ordained and established." Clearly no one had a right to counsel the ruler; only those who had the confidence of the king rose to the rank of "senator."

Since we have nothing like minutes for the meetings of the council, we know little of its procedures. The king apparently called his advisers at will. When a matter of great importance could be foreseen, he attempted to summon advisers from various parts of the realm. If an urgent issue arose, he relied on the advice of only the few who were at court. Hincmar wrote that Charlemagne "always was careful to have near him three or four of his best advisers" to aid him in making unexpected decisions and in deciding the worth of ideas that might enter his head day or night. Meetings of the council were held in secret. Those attending were expected to know about problems under discussion. Their knowledge did not usually derive from bulky dossiers prepared by underlings but from intimate personal knowledge of the affairs of the realm. The king apparently stated the nature of the problem in question and sometimes made clear his ideas on its resolution. Then he invited his counselors to speak their minds. He could accept the advice of his "senators" or reject it. In some cases a meeting of the king and his "senators" terminated with the compilation, at least in rough draft, of a document embodying the decision taken.

Although the kings might act directly to carry out their decisions, they usually sought to gain public assent to major decisions by summoning an assembly, called a *placitum* or *conventum*. These impressive meetings evolved from an ancient Germanic institution, the *Campus Martius*, which was the gathering of the warriors before their chief as the first step of a military campaign. In the age of Charlemagne the assemblies retained a military flavor, often being called just prior to an expedition and attended by those destined to participate in the campaign. The ancient purpose of the meeting was, however, expanded and modified to make the assemblies useful in all aspects of political life. The Carolingians regularly convened at least one major assembly a year, usually between May and August, at a place of the king's choice. Custom dictated that the assemblies were open to all freemen. In practice, those of the age of Charlemagne were composed of a relatively small number of great lay and ecclesiastical figures specifically commanded by royal letter to appear at the designated time and place; these notables apparently spoke for "the people."

Since the assemblies were not called to initiate programs inspired by the wishes of those attending but to approve what was already decided by the king and his "senators," their operation depended on royal management. From a long description by Hincmar and from the records of certain assemblies it is possible to reconstruct the main procedures followed at a typical *placitum*. Upon receiving the royal summons the great magnates converged on Aix or whatever other meeting place was designated, bringing with them numerous retainers, whose presence greatly enlivened the scene. If the weather was fine, meetings were held outside; otherwise assembly halls were arranged in the various buildings of the palace complex. In either case the great men were carefully segregated from the multitude so that they might deliberate without interference. Provisions were made so that the chief ecclesiastical figures could meet apart from the lay magnates and so that the two groups could join if they wished.

The assembled magnates were given the agenda prepared by the king containing items which "he had discovered by the inspiration of God or which had been suggested to him from all quarters since their departure." Hincmar says that deliberations proceeded "for a day or for two days or for three days, depending on the weight of things," without the king being present; other sources, however, indicate that he often attended as presiding officer and that he entered the discussions and helped make decisions. Hincmar indicates that while the deliberations of the magnates proceeded, the king "mingled with the crowd, received gifts, greeted nobles, conversed with those whom he saw rarely, offered his condolences to the aged, rejoiced with the younger, and occupied himself with other similar matters both spiritual and secular." All the while the magnates were dispatching messengers to the king and receiving his replies to guide their deliberations. Finally "the result of their deliberation on each point [submitted to them by the king] was taken to the glorious king and placed in his sacred view." The final act of the assembly was the proclamation of the decisions of the king and his magnates to the entire throng of great and lesser figures gathered in a public place. The king often announced the decisions in person, his spoken word being in effect an order to his people to obey what he commanded. Probably the crowd indicated approval by shouting or beating on shields. Then the king dismissed the assemblage, hoping that those attending would remember when they got home what they had agreed to do and would communicate the king's wishes to their compatriots with some enthusiasm.

Now it remained to execute the royal will. Although a special written order addressed to the parties involved might dispose of matters of a private character, the king sought to enact those decisions affecting the entire population by sending to his local agents a set of orders proclaiming his intentions. Such orders were called capitularies, which a modern authority has defined as "those acts of power whose text was divided into articles (*capitulum*) and which the

113

Frankish monarchs of the Carolingian dynasty employed to assure the publication of legislative and administrative measures. To simplify—to an excess—one might say that they were royal ordinances divided into chapters." Usually the local officials arranged for a public reading of the capitularies at a local assembly; perhaps they also explained the capitularies to assure that their provisions were understood. In one case the king ordered that his *missi* see "that the people be questioned concerning the capitularies which had been recently added to the laws, and, in order that each shall give his approval, all will sign and confirm their accord by putting their hands on the document." That the royal orders be read publicly and consented to was an important matter, for it was upon hearing the king's word, his oral command, that rested the responsibility of obedience.

Once the king had commanded his local officials to carry out his decisions and had ordered his subjects to obey, the fate of his program rested primarily on the willingness of the counts and bishops to transcend private interests for a larger public duty and of the royal vassals to abide by their pledges of loyalty to their lord. There was no elaborate administrative machinery interposed between the ruler as lawmaker and the local agents of the king for the purpose of securing the orderly execution of the decisions of the central authority. Charlemagne and Louis made a strenuous effort to supervise local authorities and assure the observance of royal commands. Their chief instrumentality was the employment of the *missi dominici* as extraordinary executive and judicial agents commissioned to enact the royal will. Surviving orders given to the *missi* to guide their administrative and judicial efforts indicate that they concerned themselves with everything of a political nature embraced by royal power. A royal order of 806 says: "Let each one have the great care in his territory for providing, ordering, and executing according to the will of God and our orders." One theme dominates all the instructions to the *missi:* their task was to check on the conduct of other officials, to correct any difficulties arising from their incompetence, negligence, or corruption, and to improve on what was already being done tolerably well. Obviously, the exercise of the royal will depended to a considerable extent on the zeal, loyalty, and competence of the *missi.*

Having followed Carolingian political processes to the level of local enforcement, we are led to a final question. What were the particular issues that most often occupied the royal government in its dedication to the establishment "of good order according to the scales of righteousness?" Indeed this is a crucial point, for the quality of any political system emerges only from its particular actions. The answer to this question lies in an extensive but badly organized body of legislation called the capitularies. A few generalizations derived from the rich particulars of this material will serve to indicate what Charlemagne and Louis believed was essential to right order in a Christian society and will help to illuminate the spirit of the political system centered at Aix.

As a starting point in the quest for order the Carolingians tried to establish an effective bond between ruler and people, a concrete tie to bring men who lived in a fragmented society to accept the obligation of obeying the king. To some degree the rulers could command the respect of their subjects by their own conduct, but the good "image" emerging from royal virtue and success was not enough. What was needed was a device which would dramatically impress upon each individual a concrete obligation to the ruler. The quest for such a device led to the imposition of an oath of fidelity on every male over twelve years of age. The oath took this form: "I promise on my oath that from this day I shall remain faithful to the most pious Lord Emperor, son of King Pepin and Queen Bertrada, acting in all sincerity without fraud or bad intent on my part toward him for the good of his kingdom, as by right a man ought to act toward his lord. If God and the patron saints whose relics are here present in this place will aid me, I shall observe and devote myself to this end through all the days of my life with all my will, in so far as God has given me the intelligence." These were not intended as idle words. Charlemagne ordered his *missi* to make certain that each oath-taker understood the specific responsibilities implied by the oath and that breaking the oath constituted perjury, a serious offense in the eyes of God and man. Clearly the oath was intended to impose upon each subject a moral responsibility, a religious duty to abide by the decisions of the prince.

Fundamental to the establishment of an orderly Christian society was the suppression of crime: murder, robbery, exploitation of the weak, adultery, rape, spoliation of churches, fighting, drunkenness, and fraud. Lawlessness was obviously endemic in Carolingian society; only heroic measures could keep the criminals under control. As one samples what the Carolingians viewed as crime, he almost thinks he is reading the Decalogue. Criminal legislation was strongly colored by the idea that crime was an offense against God rather than against human society. This tendency to place criminal action in a religious context marks a departure from the older Germanic view which saw crime chiefly as a threat to the solidarity of the family, clan, or tribe.

To assure concord and order demanded that the suppression of crime be complemented by an effort to do justice to all, an expression often on the tongues of the Carolingians. Although some of the moralists and theologians spun out ornate definitions of justice, the laws of the kings indicate that "doing justice" had a precise meaning. It consisted of an orderly presentation of disputes and complaints before regularly constituted courts where competent officials could impose a settlement according to law. It meant that men should desist from settling disputes or taking vengeance in private, an ancient Germanic habit that bred violence and gave the advantage to the strong and the bold. Only in good courts could true justice prevail. Consequently, the kings tried to regularize court procedures and to impose upon their judges—chiefly the counts—a sense of propriety and diligence. "Let every judge judge according to the written law, not according to his own arbitrary will," read one of Charlemagne's orders. It captures the essence of the royal effort to do justice. A major impediment to the administration of justice was the confusion existing in the legal system, for several kinds of law prevailed in the Frankish realm. Einhard wrote that Charlemagne "noticed many defects in the laws of his people" and was determined to "reconcile the discrepancies and correct anything that was wrong or wrongly expressed." "He completed nothing of all this beyond adding to the laws a few capitularies, and those unfinished." Other sources confirm the inability of the rulers to remove this deeply rooted obstacle to efficient justice. As a substitute they could only try to assure that each man was judged fairly according to his own law.

Concern for the material welfare of their subjects led the kings to legislate on matters which we might define broadly as social and economic. This legislation was essentially conservative, based on the assumption that each man had a position in the social hierarchy and a means of livelihood which the king must protect from those who sought to make changes for their private advantage. Since possession of land provided the basis for a livelihood and social status, royal legislation was primarily concerned with safeguarding the existing landholdings of everyone, from the great agglomerations controlled by rich monasteries and lay magnates to the tiny tenancies of the peasants. The major problem centered around restraining powerful landlords from depriving small holders of their property and reducing them to a condition of dependency. Royal legislation was motivated not so much by any conviction that large estates were evil or that small holdings promised economic stability, as by a realization that disorder and strife inevitably resulted from the activities of grasping magnates.

There were some groups which did not fit into the categories imposed by the agricultural system. Among these were the outcasts, the helpless, and the unfortunates. In general, the rulers sought to care for this element by urging the powerful and the wealthy to demonstrate their Christian charity through extending assistance to the victims of circumstance. Equally outside the general social and economic structure were the merchants. Some historians have chosen to see in Carolingian legislation affecting trade something like a positive economic policy aimed at using public authority and resources to improve a moribund aspect of economic life. They derive their conclusion from the new money system based on silver coins created by Charlemagne, on laws calling for standard weights and measures, on privileges granted to merchants, on certain attempts at price regulation, on efforts to improve transportation, and on legislation prohibiting practices which impeded trade. Such an interpretation probably misreads the motives of the law givers. The new money system was one realistically conceived to facilitate simple exchanges effected in local markets by peasants. The concern with transportation was dictated by military ends. Most of the regulative decrees touching on commerce were intended to provide moral uplift for royal subjects in order to curb practices which disturbed the public order. For example, laws prohibiting usury and speculation in food in times of shortage equated these practices with the sins of avarice and greed.

If the Carolingians had any positive economic program intended to ameliorate the all too prevalent poverty, it consisted of encouraging more skillful exploitation of the land in such a way as to avoid moral offense and social disturbance. Their model for enriching society is contained in the famous *Capitulare de villis,* issued by Charlemagne to guide those responsible for exploiting royal estates. From its numerous provisions emerges clearly the impression that Charlemagne saw the economic welfare of his people primarily in terms of a careful, industrious exploitation of the

land by the *landlord*. If all did their duty within the framework of a large estate, then material wants would be supplied and order and harmony maintained. The state's only
role was to restrain those who disturbed the efforts of the
landowner to organize his *familia* for the efficient exploitation of his estate.

A never ending concern of Carolingian legislation was
warfare. The Carolingian Army was essentially a Germanic
institution, consisting in theory of all freemen who had a
hereditary obligation to appear at the command of their
chief and fight at their own expense. Military legislation
concentrated primarily on assuring that royal subjects
would answer promptly the command to join the host,
would appear outfitted with the proper tools of war, and
would conduct themselves honorably in the course of the
campaigns. The king had also to concern himself with the
acquisition of whatever resources he needed to supplement
the military supplies provided by each individual.

To sustain their various activities the rulers had to concern themselves with the problem of income. In theory
they had the right to levy direct land and capitation taxes
on the population, but in reality there existed no effective
taxation system in the modern sense to yield a steady income in money. The nearest approximation was a system
of "annual gifts," supposedly offered gratuitously but actually made a matter of obligation, rendered by the great
magnates each year. These gifts took the form of gold,
silver, jewels, horses, garments, food, and arms; one bishop,
for example, owed two wagons of cheese each year. Some
wealth came into the royal coffers from duties imposed on
trade, fines, war booty, the sale of documents prepared by

the royal chancellery, tribute imposed on conquered peoples, gifts from foreign princes, and the confiscation of the goods of criminals. In general, the income from these extraordinary sources was irregular, limited, and in a form not easily converted into buying power. Lacking money income, the Carolingians had to rely on the services of their subjects to sustain their efforts. Theirs was a government which operated on the basis of services rendered at private expense rather than through the expenditure of money collected from royal subjects and spent by public officials. This system was applied to almost every aspect of public life: the building of Aix, the conduct of military expeditions, the maintenance of roads and bridges, the provisioning of public officials traveling on royal orders, and the construction of bridges, fortresses, and churches. Royal legislation was therefore much more concerned with the promptness and regularity with which service obligations were discharged than it was the collection of taxes.

This brings us to the ultimate resource upon which the Carolingian political regime rested—the royal domain. It was this land, parceled out to faithful subjects as benefices, that provided those obligated to perform the services vital to the state with the means to do so. It was this land, carefully managed by the kings and their agents, that supplied the court with food and clothing. Its crucial importance explains why the legislation of Charlemagne and Louis was always concerned with protecting royal lands from usurpers and from those who abused royal land granted to them on the condition that they render services to the king in return. These rulers knew only too well that royal power would vanish in a moment if the crown lost control of its land; their successors failed to respect this basic condition of royal power with tragic consequences.

Overshadowing all other matters with which the Carolingian government was concerned was one particular issue —the spiritual welfare of the royal subjects. For the moment we shall pass over the particulars of this legislation, but we shall return to it later in another context. Let us record here only that the predominance of religious concerns in Carolingian legislation indicates that the kings carried over into practice what their theory of government dictated.

As one reflects on the specific issues that occupied the Carolingian legislators, he is struck by the extent to which the political effort centered at Aix was oriented toward repression and restraint. The ultimate function of the state was to constrain the evil nature of man so that no one would depart from the norms of conduct established by Christian moral principles. If every subject could be compelled or persuaded to observe this "law" in spite of his natural inclination to sin, then peace and order would prevail. Almost completely lacking from Carolingian political life was the idea that the state had the responsibility for formulating a positive program designed to improve the human condition. The idea that the state was a man-made instrumentality, a work of art capable of shaping human nature with a view toward achieving a rationally conceived plan for "the better life" had perished with the Roman Empire and was not reborn on the high altar of St. Peter's on Christmas Day, 800. When the Western Europeans did rediscover the basic idea of statism many generations later, the Carolingian view of the state as an agency whose function consisted of the repression of the evils of which men are capable had become so deeply ingrained in the European consciousness that it yielded only under the greatest pressure.

Any discussion of political life in the age of Charlemagne must inevitably terminate on a dismal note. The efforts of Charlemagne and Louis to institute a political program befitting a civilized people failed. Before Louis' death the empire was disintegrating, and by the end of the ninth century it lay in ruins. The intense activity of the age of Charlemagne had not sufficed to win the support of the great mass of people in the empire, to overcome localism in its many forms, to create a political machinery capable of sound administration, or to provide safeguards against the selfishness of the great magnates whom the kings had favored as their chief aids in suppressing disorder. "Good order according to the scales of righteousness" was not established.

Yet the political experience of the age of Charlemagne was more significant than its failure suggests. Its importance lies in what men aspired to rather than in their successes and failures. For out of the debris of late classical civilization, the speculations of the church fathers, and the experiences of Germanic life the Carolingians fabricated a political ideal that exercised a powerful influence on later Western Europeans. They dreamed of one Europe where diverse peoples could live in peace and order under a single ruler. They believed that in compelling or persuading men to respect the law lay the only hope of achieving that social tranquility necessary to civilized life. They formulated an exalted view of the responsibility of the ruler in directing his subjects toward those ends befitting humanity and of the duties of royal officials in assisting their master. They re-established the principle that there exists an intimate relationship between successful governance of society and hard labor on the part of those charged with ruling. None of these dreams was soon forgotten; all combined to form a vision of statecraft which guided many future generations in Western Europe. Since civilized life is in part a state of mind, we must credit the Carolingian political dreamers with assisting Western European society across a watershed, through a moment of change during which it gained a precious political vision that prevented a complete reversion to the mentality of the "dark age" and that pointed forward to the remarkable political achievements of later Western Europeans. This dream was the assurance that the effort made at Aix-la-Chapelle to rule well was not made in vain.

# fIVE

## "THE SUMMIT OF EUROPE"

CHARLEMAGNE AND LOUIS were never permitted the luxury
of concentrating all their political energies on an effort to
impose Christian order on their subjects. They were constantly forced to face issues in the realm of international
politics which made Aix-la-Chapelle an important center
in world affairs. By the time Charlemagne established his
capital at Aix, the Carolingians had already achieved a
position of strength in the world scene. During the first
half of the eighth century Charles Martel and Pepin the
Short had constructed a state potentially capable of enjoying a major role in the international scene. Charlemagne
converted that potential into reality. During the quarter-
century between his accession to power in 768 and the
building of Aix, he conducted a series of military campaigns
which expanded the kingdom of the Franks into a vast
empire. His chief successes included the annexation of Saxony, the seizure of most of Italy, the establishment of a
march south of the Pyrenees, and the destruction of the
Avar Empire in the Danube valley.

These conquests created certain fundamental conditions
governing the external relations focused in Aix. Charlemagne's victories established the Franks as an aggressive
people to be respected and feared. Expansion brought the
Franks into direct contact with a wider range of foreign

powers than had been the case prior to Charlemagne's age, when the Frankish kingdom had been enveloped by a broad zone of peoples, half in, half out of the Frankish state, whose presence buffered the Franks from direct confrontation of the major world powers. Moreover, the act of conquest and the problems of defense, coupled with the more evolved political concepts of the Carolingians, intensified the question of fixed boundaries as a crucial issue in relations with foreign powers. Finally, expansion created a whole range of specific problems, more subtle and charged with significance than those facing the pre-Carolingian Frankish rulers. In short, the rapid growth of the Frankish state opened a new, complex domain in which Charlemagne and Louis were forced to exercise their talents, one in which both the safety and the prestige of their dynasty and their empire were at stake.

If conquest revolutionized the position of the Franks in the international setting, it provided no new techniques especially suited for dealing with the new problems. The machinery of diplomacy available to the Carolingians was primitive. It lacked everything we automatically assume to be imperative to effective diplomacy: a specialized department for foreign affairs, a widespread network of diplomatic posts operative in foreign capitals, an effective communication system, an intimate knowledge of the protocol and usages of foreign powers. As was usual in Carolingian political life, the conduct of diplomacy was a matter handled by the king personally. He received the agents of foreign powers, negotiated with them, transmitted his decisions to them, sent out diplomatic messages, signed treaties, and instructed his own legations.

Lacking permanent agents residing in foreign capitals, the Carolingians discovered the intentions of foreign princes chiefly through legations appearing on Frankish soil. As we have already noted, the arrival of diplomatic parties represented an important occasion in Aix. Usually the kings gave prompt and orderly consideration to messages from foreign princes. Sometimes, however, annoying circumstances impeded the smooth progress of negotiation. Foreign legations sometimes appeared at Aix when the king was absent and had to endure long delays until his return; one Moslem legation waited so long for Louis that its members despaired of ever seeing their homeland again. Fruitful discussion could be prejudiced by a variety of misadventures suffered by the visiting legation. A capitulary of 825 went to some length to point out that "dishonor of the king and the kingdom and evil fame among foreign nations would be spread on account of negligence which legates directed [to the king] suffer at the hands" of royal agents. Notker records how a Persian legation traveling through the Frankish kingdom was abused by certain bishops and subsequently complained to Charlemagne. Even Charlemagne was not above harassing foreign embassies. Notker tells that when the King learned that Greek emissaries were on their way to his court, he contrived to have them led over such a tortuous route that they arrived at Aix with their clothes ruined and their money spent. Then they were conducted into the presence of one after another royal official and led to believe that each was the emperor. In every instance the Greeks made themselves appear ridiculous by their groveling praise of the person they mistakenly took to be the emperor.

The Frankish rulers usually represented their position to foreign powers by sending forth a legation made up of three or four individuals carefully chosen from the court circle or from royal vassals. Often an individual competent in the language of the foreign court was attached to the embassy. The legates were supplied with letters to the foreign prince in which the Frankish ruler stated his position. Often they were also given careful verbal instructions and in some cases written instructions on how to conduct themselves before foreigners. It was customary also to send impressive gifts with the *missi* as a sign of good faith and a mark of the affluence of the Franks. Charlemagne, for example, sent to Caliph Harun-al-Rashid horses and mules from Spain, Frisian robes, and fierce hunting dogs. Often royal ambassadors could accomplish their mission without much delay or further concern on the part of the king, especially where such matters as the transmission of gifts, the exchange of letters, or the acceptance of homage from an insignificant prince was involved.

In major negotiations, however, involving territories, boundaries, peace, and prestige, the legates had to proceed cautiously and often were forced to return to consult their master. For example, a crucial negotiation between the Franks and the Byzantine emperor begun in 810 was not terminated until five years later; four Greek and three Frankish legations were dispatched and three Byzantine and two Frankish emperors were involved. Only the urgent desire of both sides for an agreement made it possible for negotiations to survive so many vicissitudes. The lot of a Frankish diplomatic agent was an unenviable one; it hardly appears likely that many men were anxious to undertake a foreign mission and did so only at the insistence of their royal master. Amalarius, archbishop of Trier, who was sent to Constantinople in 813 to carry on a delicate negotiation, supplied a poetic account of his trip which makes clear some of the hardships imposed on a diplomat. The poem describes the rigors of travel by sea and land, the hostile treatment meted out to the Franks by the Greeks, the uncertainties surrounding interviews with foreign princes, and the length of time required to complete the mission. No doubt Amalarius was sincere in speaking of the joy he experienced when he again set foot on Italian soil. Yet even then his travail had not ended, for he was soon informed that Charlemagne had died during his absence, a development that threatened to negate all his efforts in Constantinople.

With a general understanding of the position of strength created by Charlemagne and of the limited diplomatic resources at their disposal in mind, let us now see what kind of relationships Charlemagne and Louis established with the external world and what interests occupied their attention in the realm of diplomacy.

The various annals make constant reference to the concern felt at Aix for the Slavic principalities located along the east bank of the Elbe from the Baltic to the Bohemian forest—Abrodities, Sorbs, Wilzes, Linones, and Bohemians. The Franks were drawn into a relationship with these weak, still pagan principalities in the course of the conquest of the Saxons. The ensuing encounters constitute a monotonous record, set down in the annals as a series of Frankish military expeditions against one or another of these peoples, usually ending with a promise of submission by the prince of the people attacked. From time to time one of the Slavic princes appeared at Aix to make his obeisance personally or to avert an impending Frankish attack. Behind the dreary record of campaigns and submissions lay a definite policy. The Franks were seeking to establish the Elbe as a fixed frontier. They hoped to restrain the Slavs from any hostile action along or across that frontier which would provoke the recently conquered Saxons to revolt. Lacking the resources to man a frontier so extensive, the Franks relied on the threat of military reprisal to assure the neutrality of the Slavs. On the whole the policy was successful. At the price of periodic punitive expeditions, the Franks restrained the northern Slavs from any major disturbance along the crucial eastern frontier of Saxony. However, this policy meant that the Franks exerted little constructive influence on these Slavs.

Farther south the Franks became involved with other small principalities which were treated in a different fashion. As a result of the destruction of the Avar Empire, Charlemagne assumed a vague hegemony over a huge block of territory bounded on the north by the Danube, on the east by the Theiss, and on the south by the Save rivers. This territory was inhabited chiefly by Croats and Slavs, with remnants of the Avars scattered here and there. Local Croatian, Slavic, and Avar princes were permitted to exercise a degree of autonomy. To assure their subservience, the newly conquered territory was organized into two "marches," one of which was entrusted to the Frankish administrator in Bavaria and the other to the duke of Friuli. Under the aggressive leadership of these officials, actively supported by the archbishops of Salzburg and

Aquileia and by a considerable number of colonists, the Christianization and "Germanization" of the whole area proceeded rapidly. By the death of Louis the land snatched from the Avars only half a century earlier was fast becoming a Germanized Ostmark, the future Austria.

The solidification of Frankish power in the old Avar land brought the Franks into relationship with more formidable forces on this front. One was the Byzantine Empire. By negotiation Louis was able in 817 to arrange a well-defined frontier between his territory and that of his rival in Constantinople. As a consequence, Franks and Greeks faced each other peaceably in this area. More troublesome were the Bulgars. These aggressive Asiatics, established on the lower Danube, had for many years plagued the Byzantine Empire. Finally in 815 they agreed to a truce with Constantinople. They then turned westward to pursue the dream of creating a Bulgar empire embracing the southern Slavs. Eventually their expansion brought them to the vaguely defined Frankish frontier. After abortive attempts at negotiations with Louis' court in 824, 825, and 826, the Bulgar khan took stern measures. In 827 he "sent a naval force along the Drave and devastated with iron and fire the Slavs living in Pannonia; and having expelled the native rulers, he placed them under Bulgar masters." A Frankish counterattack in 828, supported by a thousand masses sung by the monks of Fulda, brought on another Bulgar assault in 829. Not until near the end of Louis' reign were the Franks able to recover their former position. Their effort in no way weakened the formidable Bulgars, who would cause more trouble in the future.

On the northern frontier the Carolingians found them-

selves increasingly involved with a menace ultimately destined to reshape the course of European history—the
*Nordmanni*. The conquest of Saxony established a Frankish
frontier with the Danes, but only toward the end of Charlemagne's reign did the Danes demonstrate any hostility.
The instigator of the trouble was King Gotfrid, whom Einhard accused of being "infected with the vain hope that
he could establish control over all Germany" and of having
bragged that he would soon be in Aix with an army. With
somewhat less than his usual vigor, Charlemagne threatened to make war on the Danes, but was spared the trouble
when Gotfrid was murdered in 810. Content with an assurance of respect for the Frankish frontier, Charlemagne
immediately signed a treaty with Gotfrid's successor.

Aware of the threat offered by the Danes to the Frankish
position in Saxony and among the Slavs and encouraged
by a fierce struggle for the Danish throne, Louis proceeded
more boldly in Denmark. His policy centered around supporting the candidacy of a nephew of Gotfrid, Harald, for
the Danish crown. In 814, Harald came to Louis' court to
accept vassalage and was ordered "to return to Saxony and
await an opportune time when [Louis] would be able to
give him the help he had sought." In the ensuing years
Harald was able to play an important role in Danish affairs
with Louis' support. Ultimately, Louis' scheme to install a
puppet king in Denmark collapsed, for in 827 Harald was
driven from Denmark. Contributing to his downfall was
his acceptance of Christianity in a colorful baptismal ceremony held at Mainz in 826. When Harald returned to Denmark after this event, Louis sought to promote the cause of
Christianity by sending a missionary party under Anskar.

However, the continuation of the dynastic struggle in Denmark, coupled with the decreasing danger of rebellion among the Saxons, had minimized the Danish threat by that time. Gotfrid's dream of a vast Danish empire had to await a more propitious moment. Without distinguishing themselves Charlemagne and Louis had contained a potentially dangerous foe.

More frustrating to the Franks were the raids of the fierce Nordic sea marauders who with increasing frequency devastated the imperial coasts from the Weser to the Garonne. The *Royal Annals* record that in 800 "in the middle of March, Charlemagne left the palace at Aix and inspected the coast of the ocean of Gaul, and on the sea, now infested with pirates, he established a fleet and built a look-out system." His defensive measures achieved little, for in succeeding years the Viking raiders pillaged coastal cities and monasteries, murdered their residents, and kidnapped men and women with increasing frequency. By the last years of Louis' reign the situation had become grave. Between 834 and 837 the important Frisian commercial city of Duurstedt was pillaged four times, and the monks of the Abbey of St. Philbert on the island of Noirmoutier, located near the coast of Brittany, were forced to abandon their refuge, rescuing the bones of their patron saint only after great heroics. Louis tried without success to organize a defense system against the swiftly striking raiders. It was becoming obvious that the only hope for any particular coastal region was to organize its own defense. The Carolingians had been defeated on this "frontier."

Around the long frontier encircling the empire on the east, north, and west, Frankish policy was remarkably uniform. Faced by peoples whom they viewed as barbarians, Charlemagne and Louis hoped to create an impregnable frontier. Lacking the resources to man so extensive a frontier, they sought to compel barbarian princes to accept a status of personal subordination—vassalage—toward them, any disrespect for which was cause for retaliation. Their mode of enforcement was starkly impressive: force applied deliberately, relentlessly, and brutally. To the princes involved, Aix was a city of iron. One journeyed there only to make a submission or to beg a favor, but not to negotiate. If a prince felt he no longer needed to respect the lords of Aix, he seized his sword and took his chances—seldom promising while Charlemagne and Louis ruled. Only the sea-going *Nordmanni* defied Aix successfully.

With the Anglo-Saxon kingdoms of England Charlemagne and Louis maintained friendly relations. These kingdoms offered no threat. Moreover, the Carolingians were grateful for the services performed by Englishmen like Boniface and Alcuin in regenerating the Frankish kingdom. The relatively rare diplomatic exchanges between England and the Frankish court were buttressed by other manifestations of friendliness: Frankish protection of Anglo-Saxon pilgrims going to Rome, numerous gifts of manuscripts coming to Francia from English monasteries, and active trade. Alcuin was long an influential agent encouraging amicable interchanges between his native land and the court he served. There were occasional disagreements to ruffle slightly the usually peaceful atmosphere. It was noted earlier that Charlemagne became so angry at King Offa of Mercia's proposal of a marriage between Berta and a Mercian prince that he forbade all Anglo-Saxon merchants to land on Frankish soil. Not for several years was peace restored. This episode strongly suggests that Charlemagne considered the Anglo-Saxon kings a somewhat lesser breed than he, but he made no overt moves to exert his hegemony over them.

On the Mediterranean front Frankish diplomacy assumed a more subtle and flexible aspect. Here the situation was infinitely more complex. The powers to be dealt with were stronger and more experienced. The issues embraced not only frontiers and territories, but also prestige and position. Here was the test of the right of the Franks to be ranked as a world power.

Spain provided fertile ground for adventuresome diplomacy. By the time Charlemagne became ruler, the Spanish Moslems were no longer as menacing as they had been in the era of Charles Martel. Their debility stemmed chiefly from internal strife which developed when the Umayyad dynasty, overthrown elsewhere in the Moslem Empire in 750, retained power in Spain. Almost immediately the Umayyad emir with his capital at Cordova found himself surrounded by hostile forces—chiefly Abbasid partisans— constantly scheming to undermine his authority. These rivalries invited outside intervention. It was the encouragement of a Moslem prince of Barcelona in revolt against the emir of Cordova that prompted Charlemagne to undertake his first important foray into Spain, the ill-fated expedition of 778 which ended in disaster at Roncesvalles, immortalized later in the *Song of Roland*. This defeat did not persuade Charlemagne to abandon his aggressive policy. In succeeding years he conducted a series of limited campaigns aimed at capitalizing on Moslem dissidence to seize particular cities in northern Spain. As a consequence of this aggressive policy a Frankish bridgehead, known as the Spanish "march," was established south of the Pyrenees by the end of the eighth century. Some were dreaming of even greater victories. In a poem celebrating Charlemagne's victory over the Avars in 796, Theodulf expressed the hope that Charlemagne would soon bring the Moslems to their knees and seize Cordova, which possessed even greater riches than the Avars. Perhaps the emir of Cordova was afraid of this eventuality, for during the last years of Charlemagne's reign and the first years of Louis' reign his legates came to Aix repeatedly seeking peace. The Franks usually agreed to these requests but broke the truce as soon as they saw an opportunity for new gains.

By the middle years of Louis' reign Frankish pressure on the Moslems in Spain began to slacken. The Umayyads used this opportunity to fan dissidence within the march. The chance to turn the tables on the Franks was afforded by dissatisfaction among the Visigothic chieftains who had settled in the march as refugees from the Moslem regime. These proud settlers chafed under Frankish counts and agitated for greater freedom. Their complaints reached Aix, but neither Charlemagne nor Louis did much to correct the situation. Mounting unrest finally flared into revolt in 826. The emir of Cordova, no doubt informed of the situation by "traitorous" Visigoths, "supplied a powerful and courageous army" which helped to make the suppression of the revolt long and painful. After this Louis undertook few aggressive actions in Spain. However, the march was still in Frankish hands, tangible evidence of the skillful exploitation of a diplomatic opportunity for Frankish advantage.

## "The Summit of Europe"

Charlemagne and Louis further broadened their Mediterranean policy by seeking to assume a protectorate over the peoples in the western Mediterranean who were victimized by the attacks of an ill-defined group of Moslem pirates based in Spain and North Africa. The "Saracens" made their presence felt by constant raids on Corsica, Sardinia, Sicily, and the coasts of Italy and southern Gaul. Their victims often appealed to the Franks and were willing to accept Frankish overlordship in return for protection. In spite of their efforts to build a fleet capable of coping with the raiders, the Frankish kings failed to make their power felt effectively. The Saracen menace grew steadily. As in the case of the Vikings, the Saracens demonstrated a fatal weakness in the Frankish armor—the inability to develop effective naval power.

The active policy of the Frankish kings against the Moslems in the West had repercussions in distant Baghdad. Einhard wrote of Charlemagne that "with Harun, the king of the Persians, who ruled almost all the East except India, he had so great a concord of friendship that Harun preferred his favor to the friendship of all the kings and princes of the whole earth and judged that he alone ought to be paid high respect with honors and gifts." What Einhard had in mind was a series of diplomatic exchanges between Aix and Baghdad made especially intriguing for the Franks by the gifts the Caliph sent—an elephant, a tent so large that a strong man could not shoot an arrow over it, a mechanical water clock with moving figures, spices, drugs, and precious oils. The sources say that the object of these exchanges was the establishment of "peace" and "friendship." Apparently the Caliph of Baghdad and the Emperor of the West found that vague pledges of friendship were useful as psychological weapons against their common enemies, the Spanish Umayyads and the Byzantine Empire. The negotiations with Harun-al-Rashid did net Charlemagne one distinction that he and his contemporaries cherished greatly. The Moslem legation which came to Aix in 807 brought notification that Harun was willing to accede to Charlemagne's earlier request and recognize him as protector of the Christians in the Holy Land. Charlemagne's petition to Baghdad was prompted by the actual submission of the Christians of the Holy Land. In 800, two days before his imperial coronation, he received legates from the Patriarch of Jerusalem and accepted from them a highly significant gift sent by the Patriarch—the keys to the chief holy places in Jerusalem and a flag. Charlemagne exercised his new responsibility primarily by sending gifts to his "dependents" in the Holy Land and by helping to build and support a hospice in Jerusalem.

Despite the fact that after 774 all Italy except the southern part and an enclave around Venice was claimed by the Franks, Italy was the crucial area in the Carolingian Mediterranean policy. Two powers, the dukes of Beneventum and the papacy, occupied most of the Frankish attention in Italy. The duchy of Beneventum, embracing considerable territory south of Rome, was theoretically part of the Lombard kingdom and thus fell to the Franks in 774. Actually it was virtually independent before 774 and remained so after the Frankish conquest of Italy. Charlemagne and Louis were content to accept the promise of the duke to recognize their overlordship without trying to impose direct Frankish control over the duchy. A strong Beneventum capable of confining and harassing the Byzantine Empire in southern Italy served their purposes best. The Beneventan dukes were never quite content to serve only their overlords' ends and caused considerable trouble, chiefly as a result of their territorial ambitions. Charlemagne and Louis countered their agitation by diplomatic threats and punitive expeditions designed to remind the dukes of their obligations. Their efforts usually netted the nominal submission of the dukes.

Much more complicated were Frankish relationships with the papacy. The Bishop of Rome was at once the admitted spiritual father of the masters of Aix and a political figure claiming and wielding power that touched directly on Frankish interests. The central problem of Frankish-papal relationships in the age of Charlemagne emerged from the vague and sometimes contradictory provisions of the alliance established in 751–54. This alliance involved Pepin's assumption of the Frankish crown with papal approval, papal sanctification of the new dynasty, the Donation of Pepin, and the papal bestowal on Pepin the title of *"patricius* of the Romans." From it emerged unresolved issues vital to both parties. Papal approval and sanctification of the dynastic change implied that the papacy had some part in the election of kings. The Donation of Pepin created a papal state with boundaries so loosely defined that the popes were never satisfied. The title of *"patricius* of the Romans" imposed on the Frankish king a vague right and duty to intervene in papal affairs as a protector. The weakness of the popes as temporal powers made such protection a necessity. How to mesh these interests into a *modus vivendi* that would safeguard the spiritual authority of the popes and the political power of the Franks was a burden extremely trying for the Frankish rulers and often uncomfortable for the papacy.

Immediately after his conquest of Italy in 774, Charlemagne renewed his father's arrangement. In the years that followed, however, he made his power felt much more directly in Rome. In essence, he moved in the direction of making the papal state an integral part of his empire and of compelling the popes to defer to his authority in political matters. A series of letters written by Pope Hadrian I (774–95) to his "son" reveals the drift of events. Hadrian incessantly complained of Charlemagne's negligence in ceding new territories to the Pope, of the intervention of royal *missi* in papal lands to coerce papal "subjects," and of Frankish favoritism toward Italian clergymen bent on defying papal orders. Charlemagne's expeditions to Italy in 776, 780–81, and 787 did nothing to assuage Hadrian's mounting fear that the Frankish "son" was becoming the predominant political force to the disadvantage of the Roman "father." The effacement of papal political independence became even more unmistakable under Hadrian's successor, Leo III (795–816). Charlemagne even went so far as to send the new pope an astonishingly blunt letter telling him that his only duty was to pray while the King would perform whatever needed to be done to protect Christendom.

Charlemagne's policy of reducing the papacy to political dependence reached a culmination in 799–800. In 799, Leo was brutally attacked by his enemies in Rome and fled to Charlemagne for safety. The King provided the force necessary to restore Leo in Rome, but this was no carte blanche for the Pope. Instead Charlemagne decided to go to Rome himself. In November, 800, he arrived in the Eternal City after extensive consultation with his wisest "senators." He summoned a synod of clergymen which took on the appearance of a court in which Leo appeared as one of the defendants. The Pope cleared himself by a public reading of an oath of purgation. Then came the dramatic event of Christmas Day, 800. While Charlemagne was praying before the tomb of St. Peter, Leo placed on his head a crown and all the people of Rome acclaimed him "emperor of the Romans." Although Einhard avowed that Charlemagne "so disliked the title of emperor and augustus that he insisted that he would not have entered the church that day . . . had he known what the Pope was going to do," it is unbelievable that Leo III was responsible for this revolutionary event. Rather, the imperial coronation was a logical culmination of Charlemagne's successes as a conqueror, his aspirations to be the protector of the "Christian people," and his quest for prestige. Among all the considerations making the imperial title desirable and even necessary was his previously equivocal position in Rome. The new title bestowed on him precise rights of sovereignty over Rome and its environs clearly established by ancient custom and much more specific than those embraced by the vague title of "*patricius* of the Romans." The popes now had a political master whose powers over Rome were as complete as those of the Byzantine emperors whom the popes had repudiated half a century earlier in favor of the rising Carolingians.

After 800 the emperors usually exercised their sovereignty in Rome effectively. Charlemagne's agents acted in the papal state without papal approval, while papal complaints were given little more than perfunctory attention at Aix. Louis relaxed this policy briefly during the early part of his reign. However, serious disturbances in Rome in 824 caused him to reconsider his earlier leniency and to impose a new set of regulations defining Frankish-papal relations. He ordained a machinery to give an annual accounting to Louis of the administration of the papal state. He insisted upon imperial approval of papal elections before the consecration of a new pope. The right of the emperor to intervene in any matter in Rome where the pope did not give full satisfaction was clearly affirmed. Charlemagne would surely have approved of this restoration of full Frankish sovereignty over Rome. The general policy of Charlemagne and Louis in no sense meant that the Frankish emperors nourished hostility toward the papacy; the emperors showed on many occasions their acceptance of and respect for the pope's spiritual authority. Nor did the popes chafe too much under a regime that gave them greater security than ever in Rome. But there was no mistaking that the emperors had interpreted their duty to protect their spiritual fathers in a way which deprived Peter's successors of nearly all political power. Already there were prefigured the great issues destined to occupy church-state relations throughout the Middle Ages. In the age of Charlemagne the state clearly had the upper hand.

Never far in the background of the Italian policy of the Frankish court was Byzantium. Well before the age of Charlemagne, the seeds of rivalry had been sown between Franks and Greeks. Pepin's granting of Byzantine territory to the papacy, his assumption of the title "*patricius* of the Romans," the Western repudiation of iconoclasm, and

Charlemagne's annexation of the Lombard kingdom were all ominous signs of Frankish aggressiveness towards Byzantium.

Charlemagne's first negotiations with Constantinople came in 781. Upon assuming the regency for her son, Constantine VI, Irene sought friendship with the Franks in order to solidify her position in Constantinople and to resolve the iconoclastic quarrel. She offered a marriage joining her son with Charlemagne's infant daughter Rotrud. Charlemagne agreed to this proposal, but by 787 the marriage plan was abrogated because of growing hostility between the two courts. Irene's position was now established, and she was growing increasingly annoyed at Frankish aggressiveness in southern Italy. Charlemagne was irked by Greek intrigues in Beneventum. And he was especially piqued at Irene's disposal of the iconoclastic dispute. After long consultation with Pope Hadrian she had summoned what claimed to be an ecumenical council at Nicaea in 787 and issued a statement defining the "correct" doctrine on the use of icons—without any consultation with Charlemagne, who viewed himself as the pillar of orthodoxy. After 787, Byzantine-Frankish relations were increasingly hostile. Greeks and Franks warred in Beneventum, and the Franks seized Istria. In 791, Charlemagne voiced his feelings toward the Greeks in a tract called the *Caroline Books*, which was both a refutation of the doctrinal position established at Nicaea and a vitriolic polemic against Byzantine claims to universal authority. Not content to fulminate against the Greeks, he held his own council at Frankfort in 794 to define the "orthodox" position on iconoclasm and then sought to compel Hadrian to accept it.

Once again Irene tried to re-establish friendly relations. In 797 she deposed her son and assumed the purple herself. In 798 and 799 she sent legations to Aix, apparently seeking to persuade Charlemagne to recognize her seizure of power in return for concessions in Istria and Beneventum. Charlemagne received her legations amicably, but it is not clear whether he acceded to Irene's wishes. This attempt at amity was shattered by the imperial coronation in 800. Constantinople could only view this as a usurpation; perhaps Irene even expected Charlemagne to use his title as a pretext for seizing Byzantine territory in Italy. Charlemagne apparently was even more nervous about the possible repercussions of his act. This may explain why Einhard insisted that he did not wish the imperial title; by putting the blame on poor Leo III, the Frankish king might escape Byzantine wrath. Certainly, immediately after 800, Charlemagne proceeded cautiously so as to avoid fanning Byzantine suspicions that he had vast aspirations for imperial greatness. Nonetheless, the coronation of 800 provided him with the key issue of his future Byzantine policy— how to get recognition from Constantinople for his title.

Irene was apparently not long in persuading herself that Charlemagne had no intention of seizing all the old Roman Empire. Her position as empress was deteriorating rapidly and she tried to protect it by turning once more to the West. In 802 her legates came to Aix. Charlemagne quickly dispatched two ambassadors "to establish peace with her." A Greek chronicler says that these legates "asked that Irene be united to Charles in marriage so that East and West could be joined as one." Does this report—made in one source only—indicate that the lord of the West had been

144

carried away by the heady prospect of making an inexpensive "conquest" which would elevate him to the summit of earthly power? The sources permit no answer. Irene was reportedly ready to accept the marriage, but her supporters had no stomach for the aggressive "barbarian" as their master. Their reply was simple: They deposed Irene and made Nicephorus emperor in 802.

Nicephorus tried to establish friendship with Charlemagne in 803. The Frank agreed to peace if Nicephorus would recognize his imperial title. Nicephorus did not even bother to reply to what Constantinople viewed as an empty claim by a barbarian. Charlemagne then proceeded to exploit with great skill a variety of opportunities to show the Greeks that his power was not to be taken lightly. His chief stroke was the seizure of Venice in 809. The loss of this valuable city convinced Nicephorus that it was time to seek peace. In 810 his legates came to Aix, offering to recognize Charlemagne's imperial title if the Franks would surrender Venice. After further negotiations a Greek legation sent by Nicephorus' successor, Michael I, arrived at Aix in 812 to enact a scene that represented Charlemagne's greatest diplomatic triumph. Michael "sent his legates . . . and through them he confirmed the peace agreement originated by Nicephorus. Then at Aix, where they came to the Emperor, they received from him in the church a signed agreement; after that, according to their usage, i.e., in the Greek language, they chanted for him a *laudes*, calling him emperor and *basileus*." Perhaps still not quite able to believe what had happened, Charlemagne sent another legation to Constantinople asking for a written document in Greek setting forth the terms of the new accord. In the meantime, he surrendered Venice. He was dead when his written document was delivered in 815, but he died having tasted the glory of knowing that the proud Greeks now addressed him as "brother" rather than as "son," the term they had previously used to refer to the Frankish rulers along with all other princes of lesser rank than *basileus*.

During Louis' reign the friendly spirit persisted between Aix and Constantinople, chiefly because both courts were plagued with many other problems. There were several exchanges of ambassadors, the Greeks usually initiating the action when a new emperor mounted the throne. The most significant question raised in these exchanges was the plea made by Michael II for Louis to intervene with the Pope to prevent a potential papal condemnation of the Emperor for his tolerant attitude towards the adherents of iconoclasm. Louis obliged and involved himself in a long negotiation as an intermediary between Rome and Constantinople. This role was a mark of the Greek respect for the influence of the rulers of Aix in the world scene.

Our survey of Carolingian diplomacy must lead us to much the same conclusion impressed on the contemporaries of Charlemagne and Louis: the Frankish Empire in the age of Charlemagne ranked as a world power and its capital was a vital diplomatic center. For those who lived in Aix the constant coming and going of foreign legations seeking—with few exceptions—favors from the kings supplied vivid proof of the powerful position of the Franks. The splendid gifts bedecking the church and royal residence at Aix were symbols of the respect and deference felt toward the lords of Aix by foreign princes from Baghdad to Northumbria, from Africa to Denmark. To many courtiers the command to depart for distant capitals—Constantinople, Rome, Cordova, Baghdad, Jerusalem—as *missi* representing royal interests was adequate demonstration of the mounting glory of the Franks. To the counts, bishops, royal vassals, important landowners, and not a few commoners the incessant summons to arm themselves for campaigns in Spain, across the Elbe, far into southern Italy, or into the Balkans to fight Avars, Bulgars, Danes, Greeks, Italians, Moslems, Basques, and others were forceful and perhaps unpleasant manifestations of the importance of their rulers.

Charlemagne and Louis had become many things: the terrors of defiant but weak neighbors; protectors of those who were docile and loyal; openly recognized co-equals of the proud heirs of Rome in Constantinople; allies of the mighty caliphs of Baghdad; protectors of the helpless Christians in the Holy Land; worrisome tormentors of the emirs of Cordova; and too solicitous protectors of the popes. It is not often in history that princes have enjoyed such a variety of roles. One can well understand the sentiment of the poet who hailed Charlemagne as "the summit of Europe." For he and his dynasty had again put Western Europe on the world map in a posture of aggressiveness that would not be strange to future generations of Western Europeans.

# SIX

## "THE NEW ATHENS"

THE POET AND SCHOLAR Walafrid Strabo wrote of Charlemagne: "Now he was beyond all kings most eager in searching for wise men and in giving them such patronage that they could pursue philosophy in all comfort. Thereby, with God's help, he made his kingdom, which was dark and almost wholly blind, if I may use such an expression, when God entrusted it to him, radiant with the blaze of fresh learning, hitherto unknown to our barbarians." Here is charted another world which Charlemagne sought to "conquer" and "order"—the realm of the mind. Aix-la-Chapelle was again his base of operation, his center for the assault on ignorance and barbarism.

Charlemagne was indeed aware of the cultural chaos caused by the painful era of weak government, civil strife, and religious decline that preceded the Carolingian accession to power. He openly conceded that his predecessors had neglected learning, complained of the crude Latin written by monks with whom he corresponded, and charged bishops who were otherwise assiduous in their conduct with neglecting the education of the clergy. At the same time his trips to Italy and his knowledge of the learning of Anglo-Saxon and Irish missionary scholars who worked on the Continent supplied the always observant king with firsthand evidence that cultural life flourished on the periphery of his expanding empire. Perhaps those who lived in lands blessed with a more vigorous cultural life were aware of the lamentable situation in Francia; Notker tells of two Irish monks who came to Gaul and immediately began to proclaim that they had knowledge for sale.

In its formative stage Charlemagne's program to uplift cultural life was at once limited and utilitarian. In a capitulary issued between 786 and 800 he set forth his fundamental aims: "Therefore, because it is our obligation to improve constantly the condition of our churches, we are anxious to restore with diligent zeal the workshops of letters which are almost deserted because of the negligence of our ancestors, and we invite by our own example all who are able to learn the practice of the liberal arts." The program for the improvement of learning was necessary in order to reform and safeguard religious life. "We exhort you," the King said on one occasion, "to pursue the study of letters in order that you might be able more easily and correctly to penetrate the mysteries of divine Scripture." Charlemagne's chief cultural agent, Alcuin, wrote that in these "perilous times" when "many pseudo-teachers rise up . . . to endanger the purity of the Catholic faith with impious assertions . . . , it is necessary that the Church have many defenders who are capable of vigorously defending the fortress of God by the sanctity of their lives and also by their knowledge of the truth."

To achieve this limited goal, Charlemagne conceived a program the entire scope of which was compressed into one chapter of a capitulary of 789, which ordered "that there should be schools for teaching boys to read; that in each bishopric and in each monastery there should be taught the psalms, musical notation, singing, computing, and grammar; that books should be completely corrected; and that youths should be prevented from corrupted reading and writing." This education was intended to prepare men to be better pastors, capable of understanding Scripture, conducting the liturgy, and instructing the faithful.

Originally conceived to provide basic education for the clergy as a starting point for religious reform and the deepening of spiritual life, Charlemagne's cultural program retained its basic orientation throughout his reign and that of Louis. As a consequence, the Carolingian revival of learning was tied to an objective which limited its results. However, as time passed, the visions expanded. The court circle was increasingly persuaded that the kind of training indispensable for clergymen was also useful for preparing secular officials. One capitulary conveyed a vague idea of universalizing education by ordering "that on the manors and in the towns priests should conduct schools; and if any of the faithful trust their children to them for learning letters, they must not refuse to receive and instruct them." Some were swept toward even more grandiose dreams. Alcuin wrote this to Charlemagne: "If all would pursue the noble zeal of your intentions, then a new Athens would be built in Francia, except that it would be much better." The old Athens had only the disciples of Plato educated in the seven liberal arts. "Ours, however, enriched above and beyond the seven liberal arts by the fullness of the Holy Spirit, will exceed all the dignity of worldly knowledge." Here was a vision of a renaissance, of recapturing the knowledge and tastes of a glorious past, of surpassing the golden age through the mysterious working of the faith.

Charlemagne perhaps pondered by what method he "could invite by his own example" those sympathetic with his ends to labor "to restore the workshops of letters." His ultimate answer was to create a model "workshop of letters," a "new Athens," at his court. His effort made Aix into a cultural center in which there transpired a wide range of educational, literary, artistic, and scholarly activity which reflects the spirit, the accomplishments, and the limitations of what is called the Carolingian "renaissance."

One way in which Charlemagne sought to guide his contemporaries in the ways of learning was to become a student himself, to show by his own conduct how "to vie in learning," as he once commanded his clergy to do. His contemporaries attest his personal interest in learning and indicate the powerful influence of his example. We have already quoted Einhard's description of the time he spent studying Latin, Greek, grammar, rhetoric, dialectic, astronomy, and computing. Alcuin wrote to him on one occasion saying, "I know, my lord David, that it is your chief concern to love and preach wisdom, and I know that you exhort all the world to gain it." Dungal, an Irish monk living at St. Denis, spoke of the King as an "exemplar" not only in war, governance, and spiritual affairs, but also in "philosophizing." In a society powerfully influenced by personal example, Charlemagne's own conduct was vital to the progress of learning.

More influential than Charlemagne's personal striving was his court school. Inheriting a moribund institution that had been maintained by earlier Frankish kings to instruct royal children and those of a few nobles, Charlemagne acted with characteristic boldness to increase the stature of the court school. His solution was to import talent from those centers where there were teachers and scholars with experience in education and scholarship. From Italy came the grammarian Peter of Pisa, the poet, grammarian, and historian Paul the Deacon, and the theologian Paulinus. From England came the key figure, Alcuin, a product of English monastic life. His arrival at the court in 782 with a small circle of learned companions marked the real beginning of the revitalization of the palace school. Other learned foreigners were the Spaniard Theodulf and the Irish scholars Clement, Josephus Scottus, and Dungal. At least one Frank, Angilbert, played a significant role in the court school, but the chief burden in the war on ignorance was borne in the beginning by foreigners. The learned circle at Aix changed constantly. The aged Peter of Pisa soon returned to Italy, and so did Paul, who found "the palace a prison" in which "life was a hurricane." Several court scholars, including Alcuin, Theodulf, Paulinus, and Angilbert, were appointed to ecclesiastical offices which removed them from Aix. But new scholars, increasingly drawn from men of Frankish origin, took their places: Einhard, Walafrid Strabo, Aldric, and Claudius of Turin. Thus for at least two generations there was always a cadre of competent men present at Aix to sustain an intensive educational effort.

Despite the constant shifting of key personages, a remarkable continuity of purpose dominated the court masters, a continuity arising from the model provided by the early masters, Alcuin above all. What was so strikingly new about the program of the Carolingian court school compared with the activities of the earlier school was its emphasis on literary education as a springboard to true wisdom. Alcuin and his contemporaries never viewed a literary education as an end in itself; theology was superior. But they were convinced that only a literate man could grasp the divine mysteries. Permeating the views of the court scholars toward literary education was a powerful conservatism manifesting itself in a deep respect for authority. The proper end of learning was not to open new vistas to an inquisitive mind but to impregnate an ignorant mind with truths uttered by greater authorities. Alcuin put it this way: "We are all but infants at the end of time; there is nothing better for us than to follow the teachings of the Apostles and the Gospels. We must follow these precepts instead of inventing new ones or propagating new doctrines or vainly seeking to increase our own fame by the discovery of newfangled ideas." This conviction, reflecting the mentality of the monastery, imposed a certain narrowness on Carolingian thought and learning. At the same time, the obeisance to authority oriented all effort firmly toward what most needed to be done: the recovery, purification, and comprehension of a superior tradition which could provide a foundation for new and original cultural advances.

We are poorly informed about the operation of the court school, perhaps because its masters were too occupied with teaching and writing to discuss methods and procedures. There may have been a special building in the *palatium* for education, but learning activity was never confined to a corner of the city. Instruction took place around the royal table, in the royal bed chamber, and in the bath. There is some indication that the young students were segregated for a rigorous program of reading, writing, singing, and drilling in grammar, while older students were given advanced instruction in the liberal arts and sacred studies by the chief masters of the court. There is no certainty, however, that instruction progressed in so formal a fashion; some evidence suggests a chaotic situation. In one of his poems Alcuin pictures a scene in which one teacher instructs a group of youngsters in sacred singing while a grammarian holds a class in versification. Over all this booms the voice of a theologian addressing young clerics. Both Alcuin and Archbishop Arn of Salzburg wrote to a student named Dodo, familiarly called "Cuckoo," to warn him against waywardness. In a poem Alcuin says it would be sad "if Bacchus, who snatches youths into a foul pit, drowned the Cuckoo in the depths." On other occasions Alcuin cautioned his disciples against the snares of wealth, fame, and sensuousness that might entrap them at court. All of this suggests that strict discipline and rigorous organization were not characteristic of the court school—and that student inclinations have changed little across the ages.

Somewhat more precise is our information about the method and the material used to provide a literary education. Our best sources are the textbooks compiled by Alcuin. Like most textbooks, these manuals are hardly lively, but they reveal the mentality, the aims, and the methods of the court scholars as surely as do most textbooks.

The prevailing method of instruction is described in a sentence from Alcuin's *On Rhetoric:* "To question wisely is to teach." Instead of the master's presenting a formal exposition of his material, the student either posed set questions which the master answered or he responded to the master's questions. In his *On Grammar*, Alcuin has a younger student questioning an older one. The method can best be illustrated by a few examples from the questions included in a brief work entitled *Dialogue Between the Most Noble and Royal Youth Pepin and Master Alcuin,* in which Alcuin is shown instructing the son of Charlemagne:

*Pepin:* What is a letter?
*Alcuin:* The keeper of history.
*P:* What is speech?
*A:* The revealer of the soul.
*P:* What brings forth speech?
*A:* The tongue.
*P:* What is the tongue?
*A:* The whip of the air.
*P:* What is air?
*A:* The guardian of life . . . .
*P:* What is the brain?
*A:* The conserver of memory . . . .
*P:* What is the wind?
*A:* The stirrer of the air, the mover of the waters, the dryer of the earth . . . .

After continuing in this vein through many subjects, Alcuin confronts his pupil with such riddles as these:

*Alcuin:* I have seen dead things give life, and living things consumed to death by the living.
*Pepin:* It is fire born from the friction of trees which consumes trees . . . .
*A:* Who is it that is not able to see unless his eyes are closed?
*P:* He who sleeps deeply will tell you . . . .

One may question whether these examples demonstrate how to question wisely, but he can recognize that the method is intended to force the student to learn a set of stock answers derived from recognized authorities and to develop a facility of expression.

The seven liberal arts as laid down by classical pedagogues served as the framework for organizing the content of the educational program. However, the Carolingians conceived the liberal arts somewhat differently than did classical scholars. The liberal arts were a means to an end and not a legitimate object of learning in themselves. In a letter to a community of Irish monks Alcuin illustrates the attitude of the age of Charlemagne. After exhorting that young monks be encouraged to study "the traditions of the Catholic doctors," he added: "Nor is the knowledge of secular letters to be held in contempt, but grammar ought to be given them from their earliest infancy as a kind of foundation, and also the other disciplines of philosophic subtlety, so that they might to able to ascend by such steps of wisdom to the highest peak of evangelical perfection." There still lingered a suspicion that the liberal arts were tainted with paganism. It is reported that Louis the Pious, although educated in "pagan poems" in his youth, later "did not wish to read them, hear them, or see them taught." Like many scholars, Hrabanus Maurus in his tract *On the Education of the Clergy* stressed the need for the study of the liberal arts, but insisted that great care should be taken to purge pagan learning of all references to pagan superstitions about the nature and works of the gods. Only one or two Carolingians argued openly for the value of secular learning in its own right; their arguments were more than offset by those who lashed out against the danger of too much pagan learning. Most Carolingians took a middle ground, viewing the liberal arts as useful in providing competence in thinking and expression, but insisting that their pagan content must be carefully selected and combined with Christian materials to provide a suitable moral tone and content.

The *trivium*—grammar, rhetoric, and dialectic—appealed most to the Carolingians. Alcuin defined grammar as "the science of letters, the guide of good language and style; it depends on nature, reason, authority, and custom." Although his treatise *On Grammar* is an elementary work derived from the standard authorities, Donatus, Priscian, Cassiodorus, and Bede, it reveals that his definition was interpreted broadly. Grammar implied a technical mastery of Latin—letters, syllables, words, punctuation, parts of speech, and syntax. Beyond that a student mastered such figures as would allow him to turn a fine phrase. Only the reading of proper models, including fables, histories, and the works of sacred and profane authors, could provide examples for attaining these competencies. It is clear from the writings of the mature students of the court—Einhard or Angilbert, for example—that the study of grammar led students to read Vergil, Cicero, Ovid, Augustine, Isidore, Ambrose, Cassiodorus, Gregory I, and Bede. Grammar as taught by Alcuin, Peter of Pisa, Clement, or Hrabanus Maurus opened wide literary vistas to the acute students; for the less agile and inquisitive mind, it provided solid grounding in the use of correct, sober, clear Latin. Rhetoric and dialectic were viewed as adjuncts to grammar, aimed at producing logical minds able to confront and confound heresiarchs in public debate and to set forth cogent statements of orthodoxy. Alcuin defined rhetoric as "the art of speaking well," while dialectic sought "to search, following a rational method, define, discuss, and discern the true from the false." Cicero was his chief source in rhetoric, while his *On Dialectic* was compiled primarily from Boethius, Isidore, and Cicero.

The *quadrivium* was not stressed so strongly as the *trivium*. Music was primarily a matter of mastering liturgical exercises. Geometry is scarcely mentioned. Arithmetic and astronomy were confined chiefly to those skills needed to compute the ecclesiastical feast days; Bede and Isidore were the chief authorities. Some more advanced members of the court circle extended arithmetical studies into speculation about the symbolic value of numbers. Their efforts produced some airy flights of the imagination, when, for example, Alcuin speculated on why a particular psalm was divided into a certain number of verses or explained to a disciple the significance of Solomon's sixty wives and eighty concubines. An important adjunct to astronomy was a search for the meaning of the movements of the planets and the meaning of unusual celestial phenomena. Carolingian interest in science—and in the *quadrivium*—was basically one of discovering among authorities explanations for unusual events in nature. Nature was a mirror of God's majestic and mysterious ways, and it could be read by the subtle mind as a book revealing knowledge of God.

Ultimately students in the court school had to be led to the higher wisdom embraced by theology. Thus religious instruction constituted an important aspect of education. A lack of conventional textbooks makes it difficult to describe the exact fashion in which religious instruction proceeded. It appears that from the very beginning of their training all students read Scripture, learned the liturgy by constant participation, and were drilled regularly in singing. Those students destined for the clergy apparently approached certain subjects more methodically. They learned to interpret Scripture symbolically, perhaps following the model offered by a master who had commented on one or two books of the Bible to provide a text for his students. Advanced students also read extensively in the works of Augustine, Jerome, Gregory I, and Bede. They were introduced to the art of preaching by studying homiliaries such as the one compiled by Paul the Deacon. Religious education was firmly moored in authority; Alcuin and his fellow masters wanted no heretics coming out of their schools as a result of giving students too much head in dealing with theological points.

There appears to have been no prescribed period of training for students at the court school. Students "finished" when their fathers wished them to assume family responsibilities, when their bishops or abbots needed them, or when the King assigned them to a public charge. At least a few of the most talented students remained at Aix for many years to lend their talents to the "palace academy."

Besides being an adornment of court life and a source of pleasure to Charlemagne, the "palace academy" helped establish the tone of the entire cultural effort centered at Aix. As an informal group, made up of royalty, teachers, authors, court officials, and royal friends, all bound together by an interest in and love of learning, it provided a model of a society of cultivated men. Graced by Charlemagne's participation, this circle achieved a high status in Frankish society which helped to impress contemporaries with the importance of learning. In their discussions the members found opportunity to test their creations against the knowledge, tastes, and ideas of their peers, a stimulating relief from the monotony of teaching those of lesser intellectual maturity. The concourse of scholars and writers with men of affairs kept the former in touch with reality and the latter alive to ideas. The academy was an exemplification of the faith which the Carolingians had in the efficacy of learning as a positive force in society.

The court circle was painfully aware of the obstacles placed in the way of learning by corrupted texts and slovenly habits of copying manuscripts. Their concern made the court library and the scriptorium vital auxiliaries of the court school. Unfortunately, we are not nearly as well informed on either of these organizations as we are on certain contemporary monastic libraries and scriptoria. There are suggestions that the court library represented a considerable collection of manuscripts. Einhard speaks of "the books Charlemagne had collected in great numbers in his library," and on one occasion the Abbot of Fulda expressed surprise that the Archchaplain Hilduin would need to ask for a book from Fulda, since the court "had such a great number of books." Although many volumes came to the court library as gifts, the rulers and the court scholars were never averse to soliciting items not available at Aix. Lacking any kind of catalogue of the royal library comparable to the catalogues available for some monastic libraries, it is impossible to say what titles the palace library contained. One might safely assume that scholars and students would have found Bibles, liturgical books, the basic works of the Latin theological writers from Augustine to Bede, a collection of canon law, and books containing whole works or extensive selections from Vergil, Ovid, Cicero, Suetonius, Donatus, Priscian, Prudentius, Prosper, Fortunatus, and other Latin poets and scholars.

The court scriptorium was not as well organized or as productive as some monastic scriptoria, such as those of Tours and St. Gall. The fact that the rulers often called on the services of other scriptoria when they desired particularly fine books to be produced suggests that the court scriptorium confined its efforts to utilitarian works—textbooks, scriptural commentaries, theological texts, and annals. Probably these tasks kept several copyists and illuminators busy. The miniatures of the ninth century usually depict the scribe seated on a bench with his parchment on his knee or on a wooden desk with a sloped top. Close at hand were his inkwell, extra quills, and boxes for blank parchment and finished pages. The practice of the scribal art was slow and tedious, and it was made no easier by the insistence of Charlemagne and Alcuin on high-quality workmanship. The most important aspect of the scriptorium at Aix was the contribution made by its scribes to the perfection and propagation of a new style of writing, called the Carolingian minuscule. Without attempting to unravel the complicated story of the genesis of this new script, we can say that it marked a decisive step in the development of writing. It featured the use of small letters (minuscules) formed by carefully executed combinations of round and straight strokes of the pen (half-uncials). The resulting script was characterized by legibility, elegant appearance, and rapidity of execution, all of which made it vastly superior to earlier scripts. The new style was quickly adopted over much of Western Europe; its effects are still visible on the printed page of a modern book.

As one comes to realize the labor expended at Aix to provide a living model for the Herculean effort of uplifting cultural life, he understandably asks what the results were. Perhaps the best answer can be supplied by a sampling of the literary and scholarly productions of the court circle. In many ways these works are typical exemplars of the spirit of the age of Charlemagne, although they are not always the best products of the Carolingian renaissance.

If sheer bulk is used as a criterion, religious literature was the main concern of the court scholars. In spite of its remoteness from modern interests, this material reflects some of the chief interests and attitudes of Carolingian society.

The religious works produced at Aix fall into certain broad categories. First were the liturgical and disciplinary texts compiled to serve as guides in standardizing and purifying usages in these matters. Typical were the two-volume homilary of Paul the Deacon, Alcuin's sacramentary, his revision of the Bible, and the pastoral handbook of Hrabanus Maurus. A second category comprised the ever popular scriptural commentaries, illustrated especially well by the prolific writings of Alcuin, his pupil Hrabanus Maurus, and Claudius, a Spanish scholar who served in Louis' court until he was made bishop of Turin. Somewhat more exciting was a third type—the polemical tracts produced to confute a heretical position and to confront the heretics with an orthodox position. Alcuin and Theodulf were the chief court work horses when heterodoxy called for action. Finally, on rare occasions court scholars undertook a systematic exposition of a crucial doctrinal point; Alcuin's *Handbook on the Faith of the Holy Trinity*, which he called his best work, serves as an example.

These diverse types of religious literature exemplify certain qualities of the Carolingian intellect. In all of them the powerful voice of authority presides. Whether engaged in compiling a homilary for village priests or setting forth the Trinitarian doctrine, the Carolingian scholar worked primarily by collecting the wisdom of authorities relevant to his task. This left little room for originality, a quality of mind not much admired by Carolingians. What the Carolingians lacked in originality, however, was partly offset by their vast learning. An Alcuin or a Claudius could bring to bear an impressive array of authorities to illuminate a scriptural passage or drive home a doctrinal point. This learning did not necessarily result in ponderousness. For the best court scholars were careful, systematic workmen, weaving their borrowed wisdom into arguments which are almost always workmanlike and sometimes compelling. An eternal concern with the symbolical meaning of words and events is written large in the religious writings of the Carolingian scholars, a mental trait best illustrated in scriptural commentaries. Although the modern student finds this labor puerile, it brings to Carolingian scholarship a touch of the spirit of inquiry, a faint promise of the immense realm of meaning lurking behind what is present before the eyes and the mind. Occasionally one senses that the sophisticated Carolingian scholar is close to a major intellectual break-through. A modern authority has argued with some cogency that Alcuin's great work on the Trinity marks the beginning of medieval theology because in it

Alcuin insisted that man must try to understand his faith by using his reason. His work marks the first step down the path toward the great *summae* of Thomas Aquinas and Bonaventura. Alcuin may not have been quite so aware of his own "rationalism," but certainly his learning, his orderliness of mind, his concern with meaning, and his search for clarity oriented the Carolingian mentality toward the future even while it was mastering the past.

Despite its central interest to the court scholars, theology did not command all their energy. Their fascination with human activity manifested itself in historical writing. In this realm, the court circle worked chiefly to record contemporary events. Learned men were aware of the remote past, read about it from the Roman historians, especially Eusebius and Salvian, and filled their writings with historical allusions. All of them were disciples of Augustine in terms of a philosophy of history. Almost no one, however, was interested in compiling new histories of ancient ages. The chief exception was Paul the Deacon, whose *Roman History* and *History of the Lombards* were reputable productions. Neither of these works was produced while Paul was associated with Charlemagne's court, where concern was felt chiefly for recording the events of recent periods and where annals and biographies were the forms most often used to achieve this end.

The age of Charlemagne produced an abundance of annals, most of them written at monastic houses. The chief work of the era was one called the *Royal Annals of the Franks*, comprising year-by-year entries extending from 741 to 829. Although its authorship is disputed, it seems clear that its compilers were men closely connected with the court. Like all Carolingian annals, it is a bald narrative with no artistic or philosophical adornments; it makes no attempt to explain the events described. For example, the death of Charlemagne is set down in this fashion: "While passing the winter at Aix, the Lord Emperor Charles departed the scene on January 28, in the seventy-first year of his life, the forty-seventh year of his reign, the forty-third year after his annexation of Italy, and the fourteenth year since he was called emperor and augustus." One can hardly imagine a treatment so restrained by historians as we know them! The compilers of the *Royal Annals* made little use of documents which must have been available to them and would have given real substance to their work. Obviously they were not deeply interested in history writing as an art and as a discipline through which one could grasp the meaning of events, the motives of men, and the causes of things. History writing was a mere recording of events for purposes not always clear, a mundane task hardly warranting the expenditure of artistic effort.

Although more artfully executed, Carolingian biographical literature confirms the absence among Carolingian historians of those concerns which occupy modern historians. Biography was written chiefly as an instrument of moral edification. In the preface to his *Life of Charlemagne*, the classic biography of the era, Einhard states unequivocally his intention to preserve for the illumination of others the exemplary career of the most magnificent of all kings. His work is a record of Charlemagne's praiseworthy activities: his conquests, his relationships with foreign powers, his efforts as a builder, his family life, his physical prowess, his exemplary habits and tastes, his religiosity, his interests in learning, his imperial coronation. Each of these aspects is treated with little reference to any of the others. Although he lived for a long time as an intimate of the court and was a confidant of Charlemagne, Einhard brings little to light concerning the ideas, motives, and passions which made his hero a moving force in history. He is not basically interested in explaining Charlemagne the man but in creating a hero worthy of emulation. His close imitation of Suetonius colored his selection of materials, thus distorting the picture of Charlemagne but strengthening the eulogistic and moral tone of the work. The numerous saints' lives which so appealed to Carolingian tastes and which the courtiers produced frequently illustrate this same bent for using biography for edification. Alcuin's sketch of Willibrord, the Anglo-Saxon missionary who labored in Frisia from 690 to 739, provides a model of Carolingian hagiography. Admitting that his work "was written in the stolen hours of the night, because he was so busy during the day," Alcuin's portrayal of the hero saint was rigorously circumscribed by his adherence to the well-established rules governing the hagiographical genre. While abounding in pious sentiment, his biography—and those of all his contemporaries—carries a lean weight of solid, reliable information.

Probably the men of the court circle would have agreed that the surest indication of their cultivation and their intellectual gentility was their poetry. For the court was a veritable den of versifiers who wrote poems at the least provocation. The poetic output of Alcuin, Paul the Deacon, Peter of Pisa, Theodulf, Angilbert, Moduin, Josephus Scottus, and several others comprises in a modern edition a volume of about 650 pages. This is impressive considering that the authors were active teachers, theologians, ecclesiastical officials, and royal advisers as well as poets.

In perusing the titles of the collected poems of the court writers, one is filled with the expectation that he has in hand a body of material that will illuminate the essential qualities of the Carolingian mind and clarify the world view of the most sensitive actors in the age of Charlemagne. There are epitaphs of the chief political figures of the day, paeans for the rulers, religious discussions, dedication verses for books, churches, monasteries, and altar pieces. Any of these themes offers a chance for the poets to reveal their innermost thoughts on the great issues of the era. There are poems on nature: a description of Lake Como, a dispute between spring and summer, a verse to a cuckoo. Titles suggesting moral issues abound. Occasionally a title makes one curious: "Against the Jews," "A Comparison of Ancient and Modern Laws," "On the Liberal Arts Depicted in a Certain Picture," and "Concerning the Time of Antichrist." And if one tires of sampling titles, he can amuse himself by admiring the acrostics fabricated by poets who chose their words in such a way as to spell out names and phrases with the first letter of each verse, with letters reading diagonally across the poem, and with letters arranged in various other combinations.

In spite of the variety suggested by reading titles, even a sampling of the content of Carolingian poetry reveals that the court poets at Aix had certain limitations. To a considerable degree these limitations are of a technical nature. In a fashion typical of Carolingian intellectual life, the poets were overwhelmed by their illustrious predecessors. Their preceptors were Vergil, Ovid, Martial, Horace, Fortunatus, Prudentius, Sedulius, and Arator, all of whom were accepted as the penultimate in poetic art. In versification, meter, rhyme, and mode of expression the Carolingian poets were imitators of these masters. Especially influential were classical narrative and elegaic poetry, giving Carolingian poetry a certain monotonous quality resulting from a lack of variety in form and a painful incongruity stemming from borrowing a form and meter little suited to a subject. As is bound to happen, the imitators were guilty of numerous faults of meter, rhyme, and diction. It is not difficult to amass a mountain of evidence to prove that court poets are inept and to conclude that Carolingian poetry is banal, labored, tedious, and full of flaws.

This harsh judgment, which rests chiefly on technical grounds, hardly permits the conclusion that Aix was filled with pseudo-poets and pedants. For instance, the adept and sensitive Theodulf reveals the extent to which superior talents at Aix made classical and early Christian literature a living part of their intellectual and emotional equipment. Theodulf was an inveterate imitator, filling his verse with quotations from classical authors and allusions to classical subjects. Yet he does this in a way which is pleasant and effective in conveying his ideas. He had discovered a new criterion of taste, a vital discovery for a society long lacking an aesthetic standard, always a vital ingredient of a sophisticated society. Theodulf also reflects a certain aesthetic boldness. He is not afraid to apply his erudition, his precious store of fine phrases and meters to situations existing in his own day. Without sacrificing his learning or abusing his tastes, he could draw a warm dramatic picture of the royal court or a moving indignant description of the follies of royal judges. To achieve a relevance to life through a borrowed medium required considerable ingenuity and inventiveness. Finally, in Theodulf's poetry one feels the emotions of the age. Through his learning emerges his resentment at the corruptibility of judges, his anger toward men who tried to pervert justice by bribery, his joy in the presence of Charlemagne, his loving admiration for finely wrought objects of art, and his resignation in the face of death. Poetry was not for Theodulf an exercise in rhetoric and grammar; it was an instrument for expressing a personal reaction to the human situation.

Perhaps we might comprehend the emotions and sentiments of men in the age of Charlemagne—emotions and sentiments often veiled by the effort to imitate models of a dead past in a language that was not native to its users—if we were better informed about a remark made by Einhard in his list of Charlemagne's accomplishments. He said that Charlemagne "wrote out and committed to memory the barbarous and ancient songs in which the deeds and wars of the ancient kings were sung." Does this passage indicate that the courtiers were deeply stirred by the oral poetry of ancient Germanic society? One suspects that Charlemagne's interests in preserving this poetry were not merely antiquarian. Even while they emulated the grandiose Latin style and subject matter of classical literature, the Carolingians retained their taste for the sharply contrasting tradition of barbarian society. The meeting of these two traditions in the court of a king interested in both marked an important stage in their merger into a single Western European culture.

Although our brief survey measures some of the vigor of the scholarly and intellectual activity at Aix, it does not do full justice to the role of the city as a cultural center. From Aix there flowed forth nourishing streams of influence which changed the face of many parts of the Frankish realm. Unfortunately, the scope of this study does not permit us to trace these streams to the fields they watered or to weigh the abundant harvests. We should discuss the influence of the court scholars who went forth from Aix to continue their efforts as bishops and abbots, the splendid record of the students nourished at Aix as authors, patrons, and exemplars of intellectual cultivation, and the scholarly and literary works of those who built on the works of the scholars and writers who labored at Aix in the age of Charlemagne. In simplest terms the most mature cultural activity of the Carolingian age occurred between 830 and 870, at a time when Aix was slowly sinking into obscurity as a cultural center. But no matter how the larger story is told, one would always be drawn back to Aix and to the handful of men who have occupied our attention in the preceding pages. Beyond doubt Charlemagne had succeeded in making his city a model cultural center, a "workshop of learning" worthy of imitation.

Let Notker provide the clue to a final estimate of Charlemagne's offensive against ignorance. "So the most glorious Charles saw the study of letters flourishing throughout his whole kingdom, but still he was grieved to find that it did not reach the ripeness of the earlier fathers. And so, after superhuman labors, he broke out impatiently one day: 'How I wish I had twelve clerks so learned as were Jerome and Augustine.' Then the learned Alcuin, feeling

himself ignorant indeed in comparison with these great
men . . . answered . . . : 'The Maker of heaven and earth
had not many like these men and do you expect to have
twelve?' " The impatient Charlemagne was reflecting what
is obvious to any student of the Carolingian renaissance:
the painfully meager resources pitted against the enormous
ignorance and disinterestedness of most of society. The
heroic effort of the kings and their minuscule army of
learned men made small impression on society. They are
justified who are reluctant to call the Carolingian cultural
effort a "renaissance," who refuse to admit that Aix became
the "new Athens" dreamed of by Alcuin.

What appeared to be a frustrating effort to Notker's
Charlemagne had its true significance for later generations
of Western Europeans. The scholars and writers at Aix
applied a tourniquet which stopped the flow of blood
from a wound opened in the West's cultural countenance
by the failure of classical civilization and the intrusions
of the barbarians. By their patient, pedantic copying of
Latin classical authors and church fathers the Carolingian
men of learning saved the dwindling stock of civilized
models of thought and expression. Their timid efforts to
explain these models and to relate them to the issues of
their day revitalized the nearly submerged conviction that
learning and life were interrelated. Their schools, scriptoria,
and libraries established sorely needed workshops where
cultural life could germinate even amidst social disorder.
Their vigorous reaffirmation that learning was a form of
worship supplied a powerful orientation for cultural effort
that transcended the discouragements inflicted by the
troubled age. The closing of the wound saved the vital

resources from which Western Europe's later intellectual and artistic growth emerged. In this sense Aix was a crucial center affecting the basic configuration of Western Europe's cultural life—one nourished on a classical heritage, enlivened by Christian inspiration, and activated by Germanic energy.

And perhaps, as Alcuin's retort to the disheartened Charlemagne suggests, the situation at Aix between 790 and 840 was not as bleak as the King thought. In the prefatory remarks to his biography of Charlemagne, Einhard wrote that "still another reason . . . which would in itself suffice to compel me to write this book was the education which I gained . . . from the time I began to live at the royal residence. For by this he made me a debtor to him in life and death." Here was one man whose life took its meaning and direction from his intellectual experiences as a member of the circle of learned men at Aix. One Einhard, although not a Jerome or an Augustine, was still justification enough for the war on ignorance and barbarism waged at Aix-la-Chapelle.

# seven

## "THE FORTRESS OF GOD"

WHEN SEEKING TO PENETRATE the ultimate meaning of civilization in any age, one must ask whether there was any conscious aspiration that knitted together the diverse aspects of life into a compelling orientation that gave direction to men's efforts. Can we discover in Aix that elusive motif which fused all phases of life into a sensible entity? Unless the city was the receptacle of such a force, its standing as a center of civilization must be seriously reduced.

As so often happened among the unlettered subjects of Charlemagne and Louis, a physical symbol provides our clue. Whenever the people of Aix entered the Church of Our Lady, they were greeted by a scene pregnant with meaning. High in the dome was the majestic figure of Christ looking down to remind them that life's ultimate goal was to join the heavenly host. The twenty-four elders eagerly rising to offer their crowns to Christ personified the end proper to every man from the greatest to the least. Life's whole meaning was dramatically symbolized by the space separating those rooted to the floor of the church from the majestic figure in the dome. All energy, all activity, all effort must center on traveling that space to reach Christ. Here was the idea that alone gave meaning to life.

Although the distance to Christ seemed immense to the humble man standing in the center of the church at Aix,

perhaps there was no need for despair. Between the terrestial crowd and the celestial Christ, on the second level
of the church, sat the enthroned king, man's intercessor
before God and the crucial link in the governance of the
world, charged with the responsibility of guiding his people
to salvation. Charlemagne stated his obligation in these
terms: "Since we who are in that Church have received
from the Lord the governance of the kingdom, it is necessary that we with the help of Christ struggle with all our
forces for its defenses and its exhaltation, so that we shall
be worthy of receiving from Him the name of good and
faithful servant. This is not only for us, to whom has been
committed the direction of the Church amidst the wild
tempests of this age, but also it must be observed by all
who have been nourished at her breasts, so that no one who
is known to be a member will be cut from union with the
Church."

It is to Aix as the seat of the "rectors of the Christians"
that we now turn. For from their capital, their "fortress of
God," Charlemagne and Louis sought to organize an assault
on heaven, a campaign to arm their subjects with the virtues
pleasing to God and to cut out the evils which barred access
to heaven. Their effort made Aix the spiritual capital of
the West for a generation. More important, the assault on
heaven provided the critical matrix from which all else
derived meaning.

Charlemagne and Louis believed that the prime require-
ment for waging spiritual warfare was a strong ecclesiastical
organization. Their essential problem was that of strengthening and reinvigorating the time-honored episcopal hierarchy. One writer summarized the role of the bishops in

174

this fashion in a letter to Charlemagne: "Be mindful always, my King, to rule your kingdom with fear and love of God, because you stand in His place to rule and care for all His members. . . . And the bishop is in the second place, representing Christ." In a capitulary Charlemagne greeted his bishops as "pastors of the church of Christ, leaders of His flock, and the brightest lights of the world."

Royal legislation aimed at the impediments crippling episcopal administration fell into two broad categories: the excision of all situations which interfered with the exercise of episcopal authority and the more precise definition of the power of the bishops and of the procedures to be followed in the exercise of that power. Among the chief obstacles which needed to be removed were absenteeism, the existence of private churches controlled by secular lords, excessive episcopal involvement in secular affairs, lay interference in episcopal administration, and insubordination among the ecclesiastical personnel serving the bishops. In clarifying episcopal powers and procedures, Carolingian legislation sought to subordinate all the lesser clergy to episcopal authority, to impose on the clergy in every diocese a rigorous discipline defined by a modified monastic rule, to tighten episcopal control over liturgy, discipline of laymen, and the use of church wealth, and to improve episcopal supervision over religious life through regular diocesan synods and periodic episcopal visitations. Measures were taken to free bishops for more intense concentration on spiritual duties by providing each with a lay agent, called an advocate, whose job it was to handle nonspiritual matters connected with the administration of church property and to discharge episcopal responsibilities toward the crown in the realm of secular affairs. For the most part, the norms for re-establishing episcopal authority and improving episcopal administration were derived from earlier ecclesiastical legislation.

The monasteries were likewise caught up in the effort to fortify the organization of the Church. Charlemagne gave only perfunctory attention to this problem, perhaps because he lacked sympathy with the ascetic ideal. By the end of his reign there was mounting evidence that monasticism was the most neglected aspect of religious life, that the assault on the spiritual ills of the age had by-passed the sanctuaries where the elite soldiers of Christ were supposedly found. Louis attacked this problem with great vigor, ably guided by one of the truly imposing figures of the age, Benedict of Aniane. Benedict had become a monk in 773. He was soon offended by the ease, wealth, and excessive concentration on worldly learning prevailing in the chief monasteries of the realm. Out of this experience was distilled the central aim of his career: the imposition of the Benedictine rule in all its primitive purity. As a consequence of the rigorous asceticism practiced at his newly founded monastery in Aniane in Aquitaine, Benedict's fame increased and eventually attracted Louis, who summoned the pious abbot to Aix almost as soon as he became emperor. Until his death in 821 Benedict led in an effort to use royal power to impose the Benedictine rule on all monasteries. The first chapter of a capitulary issued after a meeting of abbots held at Aix in 817 summarizes his program: "Let all abbots, as soon as they return to their monasteries, read completely through and discuss every single word of the rule [of St. Benedict], and having understood it . . . strive

diligently with their monks to live up to it." Benedict sought
to expedite monastic reform by personally visiting monasteries to suggest reforms and by writing on ancient monastic practices and the Benedictine rule in a fashion intended
to rekindle enthusiasm for strict asceticism as the most
perfect manner of pleasing God. Monastic reform aroused
considerable hostility, but the vigorous support given to
Benedict's program by Louis and several important bishops
eventually brought about marked improvement in monastic life.

Both Charlemagne and Louis were realistic enough to
see that the bishops and abbots needed adequate material
resources to discharge their duties effectively. For the most
part, the bishops and abbots derived their chief income
from the extensive church lands. Royal legislation sought
to protect that land and to allow the Church to benefit from
those whose piety prompted them to bestow new lands on
the Church. Charlemagne and Louis were under strong
pressure from the higher clergy to restore lands that had
been usurped by laymen in the era preceding the age of
Charlemagne. Neither acceded to that pressure; in some
cases they themselves were responsible for granting church
lands to laymen for political purposes. They did act to
protect and assure ecclesiastical income by insisting that
ecclesiastical property granted to laymen be considered as
benefices which the holders could use on condition of
rendering a specified part of the income to the church
authorities who retained the right of ownership. As a consequence, bishops and abbots derived a steady income from
lands they did not control directly. Charlemagne took an
important step to improve the material situation of the

Church by reinstating the tithe, with severe penalties for those who sought to avoid its payment. A royal prescription that only one-fourth of the income of the tithes should go to the bishop while the rest was to be reserved for the support of the priest, for charity, and for the upkeep of the local church strongly suggests that the tithe was intended to assure the material support of the impoverished lesser clergy.

Impelled by the ever present idea that personal conduct was the key to effective leadership, Charlemagne and Louis sought to fill the key spots in the hierarchy with men especially dedicated to the cause of improving spiritual life. The capitularies are filled with exhortations to the higher clergy to take care lest their power and wealth corrupt them. "Bishops ought not to oppress those subject to them with forceful and tyrannical power, but should care for the flock committed to them with love, gentleness, and charity and by the example of good works." To assure a superior level of competence among the higher clergy, the kings sought to exert direct personal supervision over their activity. It was this intimate contact between court and clergy which more than anything else made Aix the religious center—the *curia*—of much of Western Europe.

The methods of control were varied. Crucial was royal control over appointments. While paying lip service to the ancient canonical prescriptions that said that bishops should be chosen by the clergy and people of the diocese and that abbots should be elected by the monks in each monastery, both Charlemagne and Louis unashamedly filled high offices with men of their own choice. The clergy seldom denied the royal right of election. For the most part bishops and abbots were drawn from the great families allied with the Carolingians, but in some cases pious men of talent from humbler backgrounds reached high ecclesiastical rank. Once installed in office, the chief clergymen were under constant royal surveillance. Hardly a year passed without a summons to appear at Aix or some other place for a synod. A constant stream of letters flowed to and from Aix touching on the conduct of episcopal and monastic affairs. Royal *missi* regularly investigated affairs in each diocese and abbey. Ecclesiastical disputes and disciplinary cases were adjudicated under royal supervision at Aix. Whenever the rulers traveled, they visited bishops and abbots; some of Notker's stories suggest that these encounters were extremely painful for negligent clergymen. These frequent contacts between court and clergy indicate a degree of ecclesiastical centralization such as the Western church had never witnessed before and would not see again until the eleventh century.

On the whole, the effort to reinvigorate the hierarchy bore fruit. There were occasions of gross misconduct among bishops and abbots, but royal retaliation was usually swift. The greed of the chief church officials for property was difficult to control. Since most bishops and abbots were of aristocratic origin, they found it difficult to divest themselves of aristocratic pleasures—palaces, banquets, hunting, gaming, and politicking—to such an extent that the chief court moralist, Alcuin, was kept busy writing letters warning of the spiritual dangers inherent in such pursuits. Probably Theodulf was justified in chiding the bishops in this fashion: "A bishop who is himself full of food should not try to stop others from being gluttons. He ought not to permit himself to forbid wine to others when he himself fills the goblet, and he ought not to preach sobriety when he himself is drunk." But this evidence of unbecoming ecclesiastical conduct is more than offset by numerous examples of zealous effort by individual clergymen to improve spiritual life in their provinces. Their case could only be made by a detailed review of the work of bishops like Theodulf, Paulinus, Hilduin, Jesse, Agobard, Laidrad, Amalarius, Ebbo, Arn, Lul, Riculf, Angilgram, and Anskar, and of abbots like Alcuin, Einhard, Angilbert, Benedict, Hrabanus Maurus, Wala, and Adalard. Their achievements bulk too large to set down here, but they would provide an impressive demonstration of the superior qualities of the higher clergy of the age of Charlemagne.

These men, however, paid a price for their devotion. The abbot or bishop who dedicated himself fully to the assault on heaven as the court conceived that task faced a serious dilemma, clearly described by Bishop Claudius of Turin: "Since I have been bishop, my labors have increased and have caused me more and more concern. I have not an instant of leisure during the winter to devote to my favorite studies, because I am always traveling to the palace. In the springtime I take my papers and my arms and go to the coasts to fight the Saracens and the Moors. During the day I use my sword, and at night I use my books and pen. It is thus that I try to attain my dreams."

The measures to regularize the hierarchical structure, to guard the material resources of the Church, to fill the highest ecclesiastical offices with competent men, and to supervise them closely had a single aim—to produce what Alcuin called "standard bearers in spiritual war . . . and dukes in the squadrons of Christ." This elite group were expected to serve as militant chieftains in the assault on heaven, following the commands issued from Aix in such quantity that one does not wonder why a Claudius would feel himself overwhelmed by the responsibilities thrust on him.

Nothing seemed more critical in the struggle for heaven than improving the quality of the lower clergy. In part this involved an enforced reformation of the conduct of priests and monks, whose peccadillos were numerous: fornication, gaming, drunkenness, hunting, quarreling, overdressing, overeating, participating in lewd games and songs, disobedience, usury, simony, and shoddy performance of clerical responsibilities. Along with suppressing clerical misconduct, the court tried to improve the quality of priests by a positive program. Bishops were commanded to pay greater attention to the ordination process to eliminate those too young, too ignorant, or too avaricious to give promise of fruitful service to the Church.

Dearer to the heart of Charlemagne was the already discussed effort to provide in each diocese and abbey schools to instruct priests and monks in the fundamentals of their profession. While waiting for such a program to bear fruit, the bishops were ordered to make special efforts to assure that each priest knew how to say mass, baptize correctly, pray with propriety, use the penitentials, read the gospels, hear confessions, and apply the principles of canon law in simple disciplinary cases. Preaching was especially critical; upon the ability of simple priests to convey an adequate knowledge of the faith rested the hope of leading the great mass of people to heaven. In Alcuin's words, "Silence in a priest is pernicious to the people"; good preachers "are blazing lights in the house of God." Charlemagne sought to aid in the effort to improve preaching by ordering court scholars to compile homiliaries providing model sermons for every Sunday and holy day. The royal legislative program went far to define the place of the priest in society and to clarify the meaning of a profession. How effective the effort was is difficult to ascertain, but there are grounds for thinking that some assiduous bishops did correct many abuses among the lower clergy and thereby improved the quality of religious life.

The "rectors of the Christians" were concerned with correcting and intensifying popular religious life. One task that needed attention was the extermination of still prevalent vestiges of Germanic paganism. Typical of the practices the rulers tried to purge were the worship of pagan gods, the performance of pagan rites at the familiar sacred wells and woods, the use of amulets and charms, the incantation of ancient formulas against evil spirits, the employment of pagan rites of exorcism, and the observance of pagan dietary restrictions. Some religious spokesmen, especially Bishops Agobard of Lyons and Claudius of Turin, thought this purgation ought to be extended to certain Christian practices hardly less superstitious, e.g., the veneration of relics and the interpretation of every unusual event as miraculous. Their pleas had little effect on the court, for, as we have seen, the religious life of Aix was deeply imbued with a belief in the close presence of God and the devil and in the direct and constant intervention of supernatural powers in human affairs. Thus the Carolingian assault on the cruder, more primitive forms of religious practice was only a qualified one.

Rather than the rooting out of superstition Carolingian legislative effort emphasized chiefly additions to and refinements of the formal, external aspects of popular religious life as the key to salvation. The meager stock of doctrinal knowledge on the part of the populace did not escape royal attention. The directives for improvement were hardly less rudimentary. A capitulary of 802 commanded: "Let all the Christian people know by heart the Apostle's Creed and the Lord's Prayer." In 789 Charlemagne ordered that greater attention be paid to teaching about the Trinity, the incarnation, the death and resurrection of Christ, the last judgment, and eternal life. Other sources recommended that priests familiarize their audiences with the chief sins, explain the nature of the sacraments, and elucidate the symbolical meaning of the mass. All this hardly constitutes a heavy burden of theology, but does reflect an effort to enlarge on the tenuous knowledge of dogma possessed by most men in the age of Charlemagne.

Greater concern was felt at Aix for popular morality than for doctrinal enlightenment. The whole police power of the state was committed to the suppression of public immorality. Almost every crime was viewed as a moral transgression which prejudiced the chances of the guilty to enter heaven. The penitentials were devised as weapons "for waging war against vices, and doing so vigorously, so that no one will again be led to damnable sin." Preaching was strongly oriented toward ethical concerns. In a capitulary Charlemagne made a special point that "it ought to be preached with great diligence to all for what crimes they will be condemned to eternal suffering along with the devil." Perhaps many priests were so inspired by such advice that they besieged their parishioners with highly colored sermons depicting the terrible fate awaiting the sinner and describing in concrete detail the nature of sins displeasing to God; at least this is the implication of the homilaries which the court urged priests to use in preaching.

Crucial to the successful assault on heaven was the proper worship of God. As a consequence, Charlemagne, Louis, and their ecclesiastical advisers gave considerable attention to liturgical reform, seeking primarily to establish uniform usages based on Roman models everywhere in their realm. Three aspects of the liturgy commanded most of their attention: liturgical chant, the order of the mass, and the administration of baptism. The spirit of the reforming effort is clear in the legislative prescriptions. "All the clergy should understand perfectly the Roman chant and utilize it properly in the nightly and daily offices." Every priest should be examined before ordination to see whether "he knew and understood the mass according to the Roman order." Bishops must ascertain that priests baptized "according to Roman usage." In reality, most of the liturgical reforms introduced by Charlemagne were not pure Roman usages. What happened in the attempt to establish liturgical uniformity was illustrative of the entire range of Carolingian religious reform. The court circle began by looking humbly to what all thought were the purer usages of the past. These models were then altered to fit contemporary situations and the modified products applied to the vast realm. What became standard liturgical usage for Western Europe was what was practiced at Aix; it was "Roman" only in an indirect sense.

Concurrent with the effort to improve the liturgy was

an attempt to encourage more dignified and regular participation in worship. Apparently there was considerable
room for improvement here. A capitulary of 789 ordered
that bishops make certain that "the churches of God were
held in honor and the altars were held in veneration according to their dignity, so that the house of God and its
sacred altars did not serve as a free passageway for dogs . . .
and that secular business and vain talk were not carried on
in the churches, because the house of God ought to be
a place of prayer and not a den of robbers; and that all have
their souls intent on God when they come to mass and not
leave before the benediction of the blessed sacrament."
In a homilary a preacher urged his flock "to come to church
every Sunday and when there not to concern [themselves]
with jokes and silly fables, but listen in silence to divine
words and pray for [their] sins." To correct these abuses
and dignify divine worship, the lawgivers commanded the
people to attend church every Sunday and on a number
of holy days, to dress properly, to receive communion at
least two or three times a year, to refrain from misconduct
in church, to observe fasts, and to join in the performance
of certain parts of the mass. A serious impediment to this
effort arose from popular failure to respect Sundays and
holy days as days of worship. In 789 a capitulary listed in
detail what was *not* to be done on God's days: cultivating
the vineyards, plowing the fields, harvesting, felling trees,
working stones, building houses, hunting, holding public
meetings, weaving, sewing, spinning, and laundering.

To assure dignity in honoring God and perhaps to attract
people from their routine labors and accustomed diversions,
the rulers were anxious to improve the physical condition

of the churches. Einhard wrote that Charlemagne "ordered that wherever in all his kingdom holy buildings were found to have fallen into disrepair because of age, the pontiffs and fathers to whose care they pertained should restore them; and he took care through his legates that his orders were carried out." The capitularies bear out this statement, for the kings were always prodding ecclesiastical officials to provide better facilities for worship. Many bishops and abbots followed the royal orders with zeal and established reputations as builders; the example set by the rulers in pouring their private wealth into the building and beautification of churches probably helped to spur on the higher clergy. There was at least some truth in Charlemagne's prideful statement in the *Caroline Books* comparing the churches in his realm to those of the Greeks: "We have found from our legates . . . that many basilicas in their lands not only lacked lamps and censors but even roofs, while the basilicas in the kingdom conceded to us by God . . . are lavishly filled with gold and silver, gems and pearls, and other precious objects."

While the efforts to purify the Christian flock advanced, religious spokesmen fretted with an almost pathological anxiety about the dangers offered by heretics and pagans. They pleaded with the rulers not to fail as "the strong right arm" of the Church. The "rectors of the Christians" rose to the challenge. Charlemagne, for example, wrote to Pope Leo III that it was his royal duty "to defend by force of arms the holy Church of Christ everywhere from the invasions of pagans and from the devastations of the infidels coming from the outside, and to fortify it within by making known the Catholic faith." Such a conviction resulted in adding to the pastoral work instituted at Aix a program aimed at guarding orthodoxy and spreading the faith.

The menace of heresy confronted the Carolingians in three different forms: Adoptionism, iconoclasm, and the *filioque* question. Passing over the thorny dogmatic issues at stake here, let us concentrate on the defenses organized at Aix to combat these menaces. "Defense" is indeed the proper word, for the rulers and their theologians believed that the true faith had already been defined. They viewed heresy as something "new" devised by misguided or wicked men to challenge the "Catholic faith," a set quantity known to all. The task of the defenders of orthodoxy was to stand guard against departures from an established truth. The court at Aix did not concern itself with orthodoxy until a heretic appeared or a misguided spirit made a suspect statement. Then the keepers of "the fortress of God" moved to eliminate the threat.

Almost without exception the first step in combating heresy consisted of establishing a precise, written statement of the orthodox position on the problem in question. This burden fell upon the court scholars in whom the rulers had confidence. At various times Alcuin, Paulinus, Theodulf, and Smargardus wrote extensive tracts setting forth the correct teaching on the heresies mentioned above. In the main their job involved ransacking Scripture and patristic literature for material relevant to the issue and then assembling this material into tracts which confuted the heretics and outlined the correct teaching. Their rather pedantic efforts created at court a sense of certainty on doctrinal tradition and established an aura of solid preparation for theological jousts.

Once having formulated an orthodox position, Charlemagne and Louis liked to emphasize their role as defenders of orthodoxy by an official act which transformed the concepts of the court theologians into definitive pronouncements of the corporate Church. In the Constantinian fashion, they summoned church councils to achieve this end. Typical of these councils was one held in Frankfort in 794 to deal with iconoclasm and adoptionism. Called a "universal council" by contemporaries, its proceedings exemplify the corporate assault on heresy. The bishops and lesser clergy gathered in the royal residence in Frankfort in the presence of the King. A letter from Elipand, archbishop of Toledo and the leading defender of adoptionism, was read aloud to inform the assemblage on the nature of the heresy. Then Charlemagne rose, discussed at length the spread of the heresy, and demanded that "the ulcer of this perfidy" be cut out by "the censure of the faith." Upon hearing the royal exhortation, the bishops asked for a short delay to formulate their position. A group of Italian bishops, led by Archbishop Paulinus of Aquileia, compiled a document refuting adoptionism on scriptural grounds, while a group of Frankish bishops drew up a document challenging the heresy from patristic sources. Ultimately the council resumed in full session and solemnly declared the correct belief on the question of Christ's relationship with the Father. The whole procedure reflected careful prior preparation and direction on the part of the royal circle to assure that the clergy would speak correctly and authoritatively.

A crowning victory in the war on heresy was to extract from the culprit a public recantation. Although this was an empty hope in the quarrels with the Greeks, the court applied this tactic in the adoptionist dispute. A powerful proponent of adoptionism was the pious and learned Felix, bishop of Urgel, a see located in Frankish territory in Spain. In 792, Felix appeared and argued his position before a synod of bishops at Regensberg. The bishops decided that he was in error and required that he swear on a Bible that he would abandon his error. Then Felix was conducted to Rome to repeat his abjuration before Pope Hadrian. After returning to Spain, Felix soon fell into his old ways. Charlemagne thereupon sent a delegation to Spain to persuade Felix to appear at Aix. He consented and early in 800 arrived at Aix. There followed a week-long debate between Felix and Alcuin conducted in the presence of the King and the whole court. By his own word Felix said that his "beliefs were cut out not by violence . . . but by reason and truth." The sources say Alcuin overpowered him with superior knowledge of the fathers. Felix again renounced his error publicly. This time he was not allowed to return to his see but was held at Lyons under the supervision of Bishop Laidrad until his death. Although Felix outwardly gave up his heresy, an authority who examined his papers after his death "discovered there all the errors of his old opinions." This defection was of small consequence, because long before the palm had publicly gone to Alcuin and the forces of orthodoxy marshaled at Aix.

The Carolingian rulers were always anxious to secure papal approval for the pronouncements of their theologians and synods. They were motivated not so much by a conviction that their decisions were incomplete without papal approval as by a feeling that papal sanction would add weight to positions established at Aix. Rome was not always easy to persuade. On both iconoclasm and the *filioque* issue the papal position was at odds with that of Aix, and Hadrian and Leo III fought stubbornly and skillfully to hold their ground against the pressure applied by spokesmen sent from Aix. Papal recalcitrance chafed the "rectors of the Christians" no little, but neither kings nor popes demonstrated a desire to push their differences to a decisive showdown. And there were cases where kings and popes worked harmoniously to crush heresy; for example, they acted in complete concord on adoptionism.

If possible, the Frankish court completed its assault on heterodoxy by an effort to eradicate heresy at the scene of the affliction. This method was applied in Spain. After the council of Frankfort a dossier of material, accompanied by a letter from Charlemagne, was addressed to Elipand of Toledo to instruct the Spanish clergy "on what ought to be believed concerning the adoption of the flesh of Christ." Alcuin composed a book to be used by monks laboring in southern Gaul to combat adoptionist successes. After Felix had recanted at Aix in 800, he was required to address a letter to his people explaining his error and announcing his abjuration. At the same time Charlemagne sent a delegation of bishops to the affected area to correct the situation. Alcuin, who supplied literary ammunition for this effort, reported that they converted "almost twenty thousand among bishops, priests, monks, and the people—both men and women."

The broad strategy devised at Aix to combat heresy was, on the whole, well conceived and executed. The assiduous labor to build a case on authority, the search for a reasonable basis for resolving disputes, the patient attempt to rally opinion to the royal case, and the respect paid to traditional ways of establishing doctrinal positions all reflect a certain maturity in the West. The conduct of the Frankish court compares well with that of the Byzantine court in the same era, where theological disagreement produced violence, incessant bickering, and even martyrs. With some justice the Carolingians could claim that the faith was in safe hands.

There remained the non-Christians to contend with— pagans, infidels, and Jews. Concern with their presence generated a powerful missionary movement which found its center at the royal court at Aix.

The weight of the missionary effort of the age of Charlemagne was thrown chiefly against the surviving remnants of Germanic paganism. Charlemagne's first major missionary undertaking, the conversion of the Saxons, began before Aix became his capital. His missionary policy was a crude one: the Saxons were required to accept Christianity as a part of their political submission to the Franks. Whenever a group of Saxons surrendered, they were immediately baptized, often in the presence of the conquering army and almost never with any thought of instruction in the new faith. The Saxons understandably linked the new religion with political surrender; as often as they were able to revolt, they viciously attacked the infant Christian establishment in Saxony. Charlemagne reacted by devising more Draconian methods to force Christianity on them. Thus for three decades after the beginning of the Saxon struggle in 772 the fate of Christianity in Saxony was in a precarious balance chiefly because of the method adopted by Charlemagne, a method called "baptism with the sword."

Out of the dreadful Saxon experience came a more mature missionary policy shaped at about the time Aix became the royal capital to deal with the newly conquered Avars. Alcuin was especially instrumental in urging the abandonment of the Saxon policy. Of the Avars he said: "Give these conquered peoples teachers who will feed them with the milk of babies. . . . Remember the teaching of St. Augustine: first, let a man be taught and brought to the faith; only then let him be baptized." His argument, reflecting the missionary concepts of Anglo-Saxon preachers of the era of St. Boniface, were convincing to Charlemagne, who certainly wished to avoid another Saxon fiasco. While the final campaign against the Avars was being organized in 796, a group of clergymen gathered to discuss the Christianization of the Avars. They saw their responsibility realistically. "This brutish, irrational, idiotic, and unlettered people will be brought to a knowledge of the holy mysteries only slowly and with great labor." Nevertheless, the potential converts must be instructed. Missionary priests were cautioned against violence or compulsion; their task was to win converts by persuasive preaching. Each priest was permitted to use his discretion concerning the length of instruction; however, the bishops thought that no more than four weeks or no less than one would serve best. Then baptism was to be administered according to a carefully prescribed procedure which emphasized free consent on the part of each new convert. Additional teaching was to follow baptism. The court further systematized this program by charging the bishops of Salzburg, Aquileia, and Passau with supervisory authority and rendering material assistance to each see for the missionary effort. These plans won handsome returns on the southeastern frontier, with none of the stubborn resistance and terrible disasters recently experienced in Saxony.

Louis developed a still more complex missionary strategy. Unlike Charlemagne's policy, which was designed to convert peoples brought to heel by Frankish military might, Louis' program was shaped to carry Christianity to Scandinavia, where Frankish armies were not present to assist the missionaries. His effort centered on supporting as strongly as possible missionary parties who voluntarily went to Scandinavia to face the pagans. In 822 the question of a Danish mission was considered at an imperial assembly, and it was decided to send Ebbo, archbishop of Rheims, to open the new missionary field. Prior to going to Denmark, Ebbo was sent to Rome, "where he was given public permission to evangelize the northern lands by the venerable Pope Pascal."

Ebbo went to Denmark in 823, but his effort produced little success. In 826, Harald, one of the contenders for the Danish crown and long a recipient of Louis' support, agreed to accept Christianity as a means of solidifying his Frankish support. When he left Mainz, where he had been baptized with Louis acting as his godfather, Harald was accompanied by a monk named Anskar, hastily recruited by Louis to carry on missionary activity in Denmark with the support of Harald. Anskar produced no miracles, but his work seemed promising. In 829 the Swedish king asked for missionaries. Anskar was recalled from Denmark and sent to explore the new prospect.

Louis now decided to establish a solid base from which efforts in Denmark and Sweden could proceed. In 831 he created a new archibishopric at Hamburg with Anskar as archbishop. Pope Gregory IV gave his sanction to this move and designated Anskar as "apostle of the north." The new see was purely a missionary base; its archbishop had no suffragans and very few Christian subjects. Its creation reflects Louis' conviction that the most reliable missionary agency was the episcopacy. Probably his decision was influenced by the success of the bishoprics established by Charlemagne in Saxony in finally implanting the faith among that stubborn people. For several years Anskar proved worthy of Louis' trust as he labored to win converts in Sweden, Denmark, and the Slavic territories east of the Elbe. Developments after Louis' death ruined his work, but a model had been established for the frontier bishoprics of medieval Europe that played a vital role in converting Scandinavia and the Slavs.

The vigor, resourcefulness, and adaptability demonstrated by Charlemagne and Louis made their era a notable one in the history of Christian expansion against the last redoubts of Germanic paganism. Against the often berated infidels—the Moslems—the Carolingians were considerably less aggressive. Occasionally someone ventured the hopeful suggestion that some day the Moslems would be compelled to accept the true faith, but no plans were formulated to attain this end. The Frankish rulers, impelled chiefly by diplomatic considerations, were content to leave religious questions aside when dealing with the Moslems in Spain and Baghdad.

The tiny number of Jews in the Frankish Empire provoked some lively discussion. By ancient custom, well fortified by civil and canon law, the Jews existed as a community

living outside Christian society and at the mercy of the
Christians. Neither Charlemagne nor Louis had any intention of changing this tradition. However, during the
reign of Louis the charge was raised by Agobard, bishop
of Lyons, that the imperial government was too lax with
the Jews. Piqued by his failure to get the government at
Aix to sanction his effort to impose restrictions on the Jews
of Lyons, Agobard produced between 822 and 829 a series
of tracts charging that the court was permitting the Jews
to transcend their accustomed place and to impose on
Christians in ways not sanctioned by the laws of the
Church. Because of their powerful friends at Aix, the Jews
were permitted to traffic in Christian slaves, associate freely
with Christians, have Christian domestics, build new syna-
gogues, argue publicly the superiority of Judaism over Christianity, interfere with the baptism of their slaves, and
manipulate royal *missi* to their advantage. Noble ladies at
Aix regularly exchanged gifts with Jewish ladies in Lyons,
while the husbands of the latter paraded these gifts as signs
of their influence. Agobard charged that men were even
saying that the Emperor preferred Jews to Christians.

Against all these signs of favor Agobard mustered a vast
array of precedents to show their error. Noting that the Jews
were persuading some Christians to accept Judaism, he
thought it worthwhile to expose the nefarious teachings—
"superstitions," he called them—of the Jews and to warn
of the dangers offered to the true faith. Agobard's real concern lay with these "simple men" who might be led astray
by the Jews. His solution was to reimpose the ancient laws
isolating Jews from Christians. Never did he think of converting or exterminating the Jews. "Since the Jews live

among us and since we should not treat them with evil, let us observe the rule prescribed by the Church, which is for us to conduct ourselves with prudence and at the same time humanity toward them." Agobard's diatribes do not indicate rabid anti-Semitism so much as they suggest a pathological fear in the age of Charlemagne that non-Christian enemies would undo the gains won in strengthening the faith amidst the spiritual ignorance afflicting Christian society.

Amidst all of the furious religious activity at Aix, what of the Bishop of Rome, heir to Peter, vicar of Christ, shepherd of the Christian flock? Did the Carolingians demote him from the headship of Christendom? It would not be difficult to amass evidence that Aix's "rectors of the Christians" elbowed the popes aside as the effective leaders of the Christians in the West, that Aix replaced Rome as the center of Christendom. This evidence does not, however, decide the case. It neglects the powerful emotion felt by the emperors toward the popes, their spiritual fathers. Never for a moment did Charlemagne or Louis doubt that all their striving to save humanity would be in vain without Peter's heir at the head of the flock. Moreover, to raise the issue of supremacy of emperors over popes is to introduce an issue foreign to the age of Charlemagne. There existed no clear, conscious division of human affairs into temporal and spiritual spheres. The Christian world was one where all labored to please God.

A revealing expression of the relationship between pope and king in the age of Charlemagne was depicted in a mosaic executed in a large hall added to the Lateran Palace in Rome during the pontificate of Leo III, who was certainly one of the chief victims of the aggressive religious policy pursued at Aix. In a hemicycle at one end of the hall was a scene showing Christ sending forth his disciples to preach to all people. Two other scenes were added to complete the total composition. On the left of the main scene was Christ seated; with His right hand He gave a key to Pope Silvester and with His left a standard to Constantine. On the right of the main mosaic was a comparable scene showing St. Peter seated with Pope Leo III kneeling on his right and Charlemagne on his left. Peter was giving a pallium to Leo III, while Charlemagne was accepting a standard decorated with roses. This vast composition clearly linked popes and rulers as collaborators in carrying on Christ's work, and it put Leo III and Charlemagne in a long tradition of sharing the mission originally entrusted by Christ to His disciples. Leo III, who commissioned this mosiac, must not have felt that his "son" was abusing the "father." Theirs was a joint responsibility to work for the salvation of souls.

On the ground of insufficient evidence we beg to be excused from judging whether the assault on heaven organized in Aix made any impression in the celestial sphere. There can be no doubt, however, about its impact on the terrestrial scene. Faced with spiritual disorders that might well have discouraged the supernatural powers, Charlemagne and Louis conceived and set in motion a religious program that created vast ferment. Like so many of their other programs, their efforts were inspired by the model of an earlier Christian society and their actions guided by their conviction that previous Christian spokesmen had plotted the paths of righteousness. The church of the Christian Roman Empire, of the great Latin fathers, provided their model. Skillfully adapting the concepts of that era to the needs of their age, they moved on many fronts to bestir their subjects to a better life. Because of their model and of their milieu, their program emphasized especially the external aspects of Christian life: organization, liturgy, dogma, deportment, and the material state of the religious establishment. One may dispute whether these ways led closer to Christian perfection and heaven. It is beyond dispute that the Carolingian religious effort made a tangible and lasting contribution to that institution so important in Western European history, the Roman Catholic church. Given the fluid, uncertain state of affairs existing prior to the age of Charlemagne, it is inconceivable that the Church would have assumed its historic form without the Carolingian effort. Without detracting from Rome, it is imperative that we see the formative role that Aix played in shaping that institution at a vital moment. This role in itself might well justify Aix's right to be called a center of civilization.

No less significant was the impression made on society in general in the age of Charlemagne by the vast religious program. Seldom are we privileged to catch an intelligible glimpse of the state of mind of most of Charlemagne's subjects. When we do, we sense immediately that it was their relationship with God that absorbed their intellectual and emotional energies. Especially in the saints' lives, in the accounts of the translations of relics, and in some poetry, which are the closest approaches to a popular literature surviving from the age of Charlemagne, we are confronted with the degree to which religious life preoccupied the great bulk of men. The one thing they could understand from

198

all of Charlemagne's program and could accept as relevant to their immediate lives was his effort to lead them along paths pleasing to God. They understood the need for more learned bishops, more sanctified monks, more beautiful churches, more splendid rituals, and more virtuous men; these were all pleasing to God. They knew equally well that clerical malfeasance, heresy, vice, and lack of knowledge of God's ways were works of the devil that would bar the gate of heaven to all.

The efforts of Charlemagne and Louis to breathe new vigor into religious life thus helped to bring into sharper focus what to most men was the only point in life, the winning of eternal happiness. Perhaps it was a realization on the part of the rulers and their advisers that their religious program alone had meaning to the great bulk of their subjects that caused the royal government to become increasingly preoccupied with religion in the era from 790 to 840. Historians often treat this development as an aberration in royal policy brought on by Charlemagne's advancing years and Louis' misguided piety. Their opinion, perhaps unduly colored by modern skepticism toward religion as a social force, may overlook how much popular enthusiasm was engendered by the assault on heaven launched at Aix. This is not to imply that the spiritual warfare organized at Aix made all Carolingian subjects better Christians; the surviving records allow no such conclusion. After all, as the Carolingians well understood, man is basically evil and will continue to sin. What the religious effort of the age of Charlemagne did do was to reinvigorate men's conviction that they had a new chance of winning grace. Armed with this assurance, they could live more useful lives and perform deeds with some sense of purpose. Such purposefulness helps to make a man and a society civilized. And while Charlemagne and Louis very likely did not consciously promote religion with the particular aim of civilizing their society, that, nevertheless, was the end result.

# EPILOGUE

Having surveyed the many pursuits that occupied the inhabitants of Aix-la-Chapelle in the age of Charlemagne, perhaps we might reflect on the ultimate significance of these activities in order to bring into sharper focus Aix's role as a center of civilization.

In the range and variety of activity unfolding in Aix we have some indication of the city's place in history. Intense and serious preoccupation with the great issues of civilized life—war and peace, the governance of society, the material welfare of men, their social condition, religion, the arts and letters, and the use of leisure—is what one expects in an important city. These concerns dominated life in Aix. The vigorous grappling with serious issues was not a routinized round of endeavor dictated by sacrosanct customs and ingrained habits. All of Aix's activity was surrounded by a freshness and enthusiasm often lacking in more sedate, stable centers of civilization, where the successful resolution of the problems of civilized life has engendered a conditioned reflex to the most serious issues of human existence. As we follow the residents of Aix in their labors and their pleasures, we sense the kind of excitement that grips the youthful mentality facing novel situations. To build a church such as men in northern Europe had never seen before, to send an army to a land heretofore completely foreign, to impose laws dictating a new kind of conduct, to find a book long lost to learned men, to impress foreigners from the far reaches of the world—these were the pioneering activities that have repeatedly caught our attention in describing Aix in the age of Charlemagne.

Some might protest that activity, no matter how intense or how all-embracing, is not in itself especially distinctive or unique. Their disclaimer is indeed pertinent, for cities may well be "active" in the way that ant hills, factory assembly lines, or prisons are filled with activity. Life in a city needs another dimension if that city is to qualify as a center of civilization. It was suggested in the opening pages of this book that Aix belongs to a category of cities whose importance derives from their relationship to change. Our detailed study of life in Aix in the age of Charlemagne has strongly affirmed that "change" supplies the touchstone to the essential quality of our center of civilization. It was a city where men not only concerned themselves with what "was," but grappled with the immensely more stimulating problems of what "could be" and what "should be."

Certainly Aix was dominated by the psychology of change. The figures we have met in the city desired to leave nothing as it was. Existing practices and conditions in government, international affairs, learning, religion, public and private morality, and social relations were not satisfactory to them. Their urge for change had a special quality that we must comprehend. Charlemagne, Louis, and their associates could not qualify as revolutionists. They lacked completely two traits fundamental to the revolutionary's mentality: resentment toward insufferable masters and the desire to destroy what existed as the first step toward change.

## Epilogue

The psychology of change prevailing at Aix was bred of a sober, dispassionate appraisal of the inadequacies of the existing order when measured against the presumed potentialities of men. Nothing significant needed to be destroyed to improve the existing situation; all that comprised the conventional pattern of life was raw material upon which an improved world could be built. Not destruction but cultivation of the existing order was the task of those who held power. The distinction here between the orientation of Aix's dominant figures and that of the revolutionist is subtle but basic, for it determines what perpetrators of change do with the society over which they assume power. It explains the Carolingian willingness to work patiently with what they found already in existence, to destroy nothing that might assist the cause of civilization.

The spirit of change permeating every phase of life in Aix was given a unique and immensely significant quality by becoming associated with a specific model of civilized life in the past. No matter where we have turned in our survey of Aix's activity we have repeatedly encountered a longing to emulate the civilized life that prevailed in the fourth and fifth centuries. Charlemagne and Louis envisioned themselves as Constantine and Theodosius. They expected their clergy to manifest the virtue, wisdom, and zeal of the Latin fathers. Church organization must function like that described in the early collections of canon law. Art must be enriched by forms, themes, and techniques manifested in models from the fourth and fifth centuries. Charlemagne angrily complained that he had no scholars like Augustine and Jerome. Nothing escaped being measured by the standards of that golden age.

This urge to recover a more glorious past in no way sired hostility toward the Germanic tradition so deeply imbedded in eighth- and ninth-century society. It simply reflected a conviction—one entirely reasonable and realistic—that the Germanic tradition was inferior, limited, and of itself incapable of significant growth. Humility before what was accepted as a superior manner of life was one of the refreshing qualities of the basically Germanic society which inhabited Aix and certainly one of the factors which helped to make the synthesis of the Germanic and Christian-Latin traditions easier and more complete. In the face of an admittedly superior foreign civilization, Aix experienced none of the tortured doubts besetting the Slavic mentality or the cynical opportunism of the Oriental mind as each has confronted the Western European pattern of life in modern times. In Aix men clutched eagerly and without inhibitions what they believed was superior; their enthusiasm and freedom facilitated the difficult feat of merging divergent cultures into a sensible, realistic synthesis.

The Carolingian choice of an archetype was vital for Europe's future. The era which so struck the Carolingian fancy was one in which classical values and practices had merged to a considerable degree with Christian ideals. It was the rich potential of this merger, never realized in the tragic last centuries of Roman history, that the rulers of Aix transmitted to the West. One can hardly imagine what European civilization might have been like had Charlemagne chosen the Greek city-state, the secularized civilization of the age of Augustus, or the narrow exclusiveness of the primitive Christian community as his archetype for the ideal society and had directed his energies toward reproducing such a model. The West would certainly have been different and, one suspects, much poorer.

Throughout our study of Aix in the age of Charlemagne we have encountered disturbing signs that the urge to change did not lead immediately to the results expected. The size and the heterogeneous composition of the Carolingian empire imposed monumental impediments on the rulers. Primitive techniques in politics, diplomacy, education, economic life, and religious administration hindered the execution of well-conceived programs of change. The pitifully small number of men genuinely moved by the urge to change left the Carolingians without the human resources required to leap suddenly from barbarian to civilized life. The ingrained barbarism prevailing at all levels of society imposed in the path of the "changers" an inert lump of humanity that could not be remolded quickly or completely. The age of Charlemagne thus did not produce radical changes immediately in Western European society. A perfect symbol for the Carolingian inability to effect real changes in a world they so ardently desired to change is supplied by Charlemagne's struggle with handwriting. Here was a man who exerted himself valiantly to revitalize learning in all his empire, to build a new and even better Athens in the West, but who himself never mastered the simple art of writing. Much of what Charlemagne and Louis tried to do turned out this way. In a naïve, youthful way the Carolingians overestimated what could be done. For anyone of a pragmatic turn of mind Carolingian history has a shadowy quality born of limited tangible accomplishments.

Even in their failures the men of Aix still performed a vital service to Western European civilization. For in order to effect any change, they were compelled to envision what kind of world they wanted; they had to think about what "should be." Their visions served as seeds out of which grew Western European civilization. In the final analysis, Aix in the age of Charlemagne was a city of dreams. Yet what were fantasies in the late eighth and ninth centuries became goals toward which European society labored during later generations. To build in the virtual wilderness of ninth-century northern Europe a city which would serve as a second Rome was not really possible; but to dream of doing so provided the impetus for later European cities which still to this day proudly display not only the physical stamp of classical civilization but also some part of the ethos of the classical *polis*. To institute a European political order where diverse people would live in harmony and concord was beyond the talents of the Carolingians; but to conceive such an ideal provided a powerful and lasting orientation for future European political effort. To suppress disorder was a hopeless task in the ninth century; but the urge for order and justice served to inspire Western European society toward unexcelled political accomplishments in later centuries. To think of deepening spiritual currents in the age of Charlemagne was sheer fantasy; yet the thought itself helped to determine the shape of religious development throughout future centuries. In brief, the dreams of the age of Charlemagne supplied much of the conscious orientation lying behind the evolution of Western European civilization. The really fundamental change that occurred at Aix in the age of Charlemagne was this mental transition from the idle drifting of the "dark ages" to a conscious awareness of what civilized society should be.

Perhaps this formulation of values, this collective dreaming of what the world ought to be, is the fundamental step in the genesis of a civilization.

Whoever seeks to discover the source of the values of the Western World must always travel to Aix-la-Chapelle in the age of Charlemagne. For some the course will end there; they will decide that a new order was born in Aix. For others the stream will lead beyond Aix to classical and Judaeo-Christian sources; they will view Aix as a place where the important remnants of more ancient traditions were rescued from total destruction and put into some order. In either case, Aix's brief history in the age of Charlemagne will become an indispensable, perhaps even *the* indispensable moment in the genesis of Western European civilization. For that reason Aix-la-Chapelle can indisputably claim to be ranked as a center of civilization.

# SELECTED BIBLIOGRAPHY

CONTEMPORARY SOURCES IN TRANSLATION:

There are so few Carolingian sources available in English translation that it is impossible to designate the following list as representative. These titles will supply at least some feeling for the era.

Einhard. *The Life of Charlemagne*. Translated by Samuel Epes Turner. Ann Arbor, 1960. A recent translation of Einhard's classic work.

*The Early Lives of Charlemagne by Einhard and the Monk of St. Gall*. Translated and edited by A. J. Grant. (Medieval Library.) London, 1922. Along with Einhard's biography this work contains a not entirely adequate translation of Notker's biography.

*Son of Charlemagne: A Contemporary Life of Louis the Pious*. Translated, with an introduction and notes, by Allen Cabaniss. Syracuse, N. Y., 1961. A biography by an unknown author usually called the "Astronomer."

*The Rhetoric of Alcuin and Charlemagne*. A translation with an introduction, the Latin text, and notes by William Samuel Howell. (Princeton Studies in English, Vol. XXIII.) Princeton, 1941. A good example of a Carolingian educational manual.

Einhard. *The History of the Translation of the Blessed*

*Martyrs of Christ, Marcellinus and Peter*. English version by Barrett Wendell. Cambridge, Mass., 1926. A description of the translation of relics illustrating the powerful emotions stirred by such an event.

Grieve, Alexander. *Willibrord, Missionary in the Netherlands, 691–739. Including a Translation of the Vita Willibrordi by Alcuin*. London, 1923. A typical Carolingian saint's life.

Allen, Philip Schyler. *The Romanesque Lyric; Studies in Its Background and Development from Petronius to the Cambridge Songs*, 50–1050; with renderings into English by Howard Mumford Jones. Chapel Hill, 1928.

Waddell, Helen. *Mediaeval Latin Lyrics*. Fifth edition, New York, 1948. This and the preceding title include a few translations of Carolingian poetry.

"Selection from the Laws of Charles the Great," edited by Dana Carleton Monro in *Translations and Reprints from the Original Sources of European History*, Vol. VI, No. 5. Philadelphia, 1900. Includes material on Charlemagne's educational program and the important instruction to the *missi* of 802.

*Medieval Handbooks of Penance*. A translation . . . by John T. McNeill and Helena M. Gamer. (Records of Civilization. Sources and Studies, No. XXIX.) New York, 1939. Contains material illustrative of church discipline in the age of Charlemagne.

Easton, Stewart C., and Helene Wieruszowski. *The Era of Charlemagne: Frankish State and Society*. (An Anvil Original.) Princeton, c.1961. Almost one-half of this volume contains materials of a wide variety illustrating Carolingian life and institutions. Most of the selections are short.

BACKGROUND TO CAROLINGIAN HISTORY:

Pirenne, Henri. *Mohammed and Charlemagne.* Translated by Bernard Miall. New edition, New York and London, 1955. (Reprinted in a Meridian paperback, 1957.) This book revolutionized the study of the early Middle Ages by propounding the thesis that it was the Moslem intrusion into the western Mediterranean in the eighth century which really ended the Roman Empire and marked the beginning of medieval culture.

Moss, H. St. L. B. *The Birth of the Middle Ages, 395–814.* Oxford, 1935. A readable, sound summary of the history of the early Middle Ages.

Dawson, Christopher. *The Making of Europe: An Introduction to the History of European Unity.* London, 1932. (Reprinted in a Meridian paperback, 1956.) A stimulating interpretation of the early Middle Ages stressing especially the creative role of religion.

Ostrogorsky, G. *History of the Byzantine State.* Translated by Joan Hussey. Oxford, 1956; New Brunswick, N. J., 1957. The best survey of Byzantine history.

Hitti, Philip K. *History of the Arabs from the Earliest Times to the Present.* Seventh edition, New York and London, 1960. An excellent survey of the rise of the Moslem empire and of its civilization.

Sullivan, Richard E. *Heirs of the Roman Empire.* Ithaca, N. Y., c.1960. An attempt to show the relationship between Byzantine, Moslem, and Western European civilizations between 600 and 900.

ART OF AIX-LA-CHAPELLE:

Conant, Kenneth John. *Carolingian and Romanesque*

*Architecture, 800 to 1200.* (The Pelican History of Art, Vol. XIII). Harmondsworth, Eng., 1959. The opening chapters provide an excellent introduction to Carolingian architecture.

Morey, Charles Rufus. *Mediaeval Art.* New York, 1942. A good treatment of Carolingian painting and sculpture and their antecedants.

Hinks, Roger. *Carolingian Art.* London, 1935. A detailed study throwing considerable light on the technical features of Carolingian art.

Haupt, Albrecht. *Die Pfalzkapelle Kaiser Karls des Grossen zu Aachen.* (*Monumenta Germaniae Architectonica,* II). Leipzig, 1913. Contains an indispensable set of illustrations of the church at Aix. Some of Haupt's conjectures concerning the original form of the structure need correction in the light of recent scholarship.

Goldschmidt, Adolph. *German Illumination.* 2 vols. Florence and New York, 1928.

Koehler, Wilhelm. *Die karolingischen Miniaturen,* II: *Die Hofschule Karls des Grossen.* 2 vols. Berlin, 1958. These two works, both copiously illustrated, supply an excellent visual introduction to Carolingian book illumination.

Goldschmidt, Adolph. *Die Elfenbeinskulpturen aus der Zeit der karolingischen und sächsischen Kaiser, VIII.-XI. Jahrhundert.* 2 vols. Berlin, 1914–18. The fundamental work on Carolingian ivories, with many illustrations.

POLITICAL HISTORY:

*The Cambridge Medieval History,* Vols. II–III. Cambridge, Eng., and New York, 1913, 1922 (reprinted with corrections). The appropriate chapters in these two volumes provide the only extensive study of Carolingian political history in English.

Halphen, Louis. *Charlemagne et l'empire carolingien.* Nouvelle édition, revue et corigée (*L'évolution de l'humanité,* Vol. XXXIII). Paris, 1949. The best study of Carolingian political development.

Fichtenau, Heinrich. *The Carolingian Empire.* Translated by Peter Munz. Oxford, 1957. Written to correct the overromanticization of Carolingian history, this work contains provocative remarks about political ideas and practices.

Winston, Richard. *Charlemagne: From the Hammer to the Cross.* Indianapolis, 1954. (Reprinted in a Vintage paperback, 1960.) Although open to criticism in places, this biography supplies a good survey of the reign of Charlemagne. It should be supplemented by the two following biographies in French.

Kleinclausz, A. *Charlemagne.* Paris, 1934.

Calmette, J. *Charlemagne. Sa vie et son oeuvre.* Paris, 1945.

ECONOMIC AND SOCIAL INSTITUTIONS:

Latouche, Robert. *The Birth of Western Economy: Economic Aspects of the Dark Ages.* Translated by E. M. Wilkinson. New York, 1961. A provocative treatment of the evolution of economic life in the early Middle Ages.

*The Cambridge Economic History of Europe from the Decline of the Roman Empire.* Edited by J. H. Clapham and Eileen Power. Vol. I: *The Agrarian Life of the Middle Ages.* Cambridge, Eng., 1942. A detailed treatment of agricultural institutions.

Ganshof, F. L. *Feudalism*. Translated by Philip Grierson. Second English edition. (Harper Torchbook) New York, 1961. This study provides a clear description of the legal aspects of feudalism and of the importance of the Carolingian age in the evolution of feudalism.

Bloch, Marc. *Feudal Society*. Translated by L. A. Manyon. Chicago, 1961. A fundamental study of feudal institutions by one of the greatest medievalists of the twentieth century.

LITERATURE AND LEARNING:

Laistner, M. L. W. *Thought and Letters in Western Europe, A.D. 500 to 900*. New edition, revised, Ithaca, N. Y., 1957. The indispensable work in English on the Carolingian renaissance and its antecedents.

Schnürer, Gustav. *Church and Culture in the Middle Ages*, Vol. I. Translated by George J. Undreiner. Patterson, N. J., 1956. A stimulating discussion of the formation of ideas in the early Middle Ages.

Gilson, Étienne. *History of Christian Philosophy in the Middle Ages*. New York, 1955. The opening chapters supply a sound survey of Carolingian theological works, their antecedents, and their philosophical implications.

Raby, F. J. E. A *History of Christian-Latin Poetry from the Beginnings to the Close of the Middle Ages*. Second edition, Oxford, 1953.

Raby, F. J. E. A *History of Secular Latin Poetry in the Middle Ages*. 2 vols. Oxford, 1934. These two works supply a thorough discussion of Carolingian poetry.

Duckett, Eleanor Shipley. *Alcuin, Friend of Charlemagne: His World and His Work*. New York, 1951. An excellent

biography introducing the reader to most aspects of Carolingian intellectual life.

CHURCH HISTORY:

Latourette, Kenneth Scott. *A History of Christianity*. New
York, 1953. Contains a brief but excellent section on
religious life in the early Middle Ages with excellent bib-
liographies.

Hughes, Philip. *A History of the Church*, Vol. II. Revised
edition, London and New York, 1948. A more detailed
treatment of Carolingian church history.

Daniel-Rops, H. *The Church in the Dark Ages*. Translated
by Audrey Butler. New York, 1959. A survey of church
history graced with abundant illustrative material.

Amann, Émile. *L'époque carolingienne. (Histoire de l'église
depuis les origines jusqu'à nos jours,* publ. par A. Fliche et
V. Martin, Vol. VI.) Paris, 1937. The fundamental work
on Carolingian church history.

Hauck, Albert. *Kirchengeschichte Deutschlands*, Vol. II.
Fifth edition, Leipzig, 1935. A "classic" work, thoroughly
grounded in the sources.

Ullmann, Walter. *The Growth of Papal Government in
the Middle Ages: A Study in the Ideological Relation of
Clerical to Lay Power*. London, 1955. A stimulating but
debatable interpretation of church-state relations in the
early Middle Ages.

# INDEX

# Index

# Index

# Index

# Index

Theodrada, daughter of Charlemagne: 66
Theodulf: 51, 72, 75, 76, 77, 136, 152, 162, 166, 168, 169, 179, 180, 187
Theology: 85, 153, 158–59, 163–64, 183, 186–91; *see also* Church
Toledo: 188, 190
Tours: 20, 161; "battle" of, 9
Trier: 88, 129
Turin: 152, 162, 180, 182

Umayyad dynasty: 10, 85, 135, 136, 138
Urgel: 189
Usury: 119
Utrecht psalter: 54

Vassals, royal: 38, 103–105, 114, 147
*Vassi dominici:* 103–105
Venice: 3, 39, 138, 145, 146
Vikings: 62, 133, 137
Visigoths: 136

Wala, cousin of Charlemagne: 71, 180
Walafrid Strabo: 148, 152
Warfare: provisions for, 120
Weights and measures: 119
Willibrord, St.: 24, 166
Wilzes: 129

Zacharius, Pope: 19